MAKE BLACKOUT POETRY

ACTIVIST EDITION

ABRAMS NOTERIE, NEW YORK

THE UNANIMOUS

DECLARATION

OF

U   S

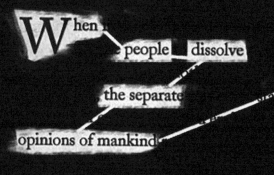

When   becomes

people   dissolve

the separate   me

opinions of mankind

We

are

unalienable   and   all

just power

is the Right of the People

wer

light

suffer,

the

train of abuses and usurpations, pursuing

FOREWORD

Whenever I teach blackout poetry to a group of new students, one question almost always rears its head. *What is it? A type of poem? A piece of visual art?* For fledgling practitioners, this uncertainty of what blackout poetry actually is can rise up as two seemingly insurmountable obstacles. *How do I make blackout poetry if I have never written a poem? How do I make blackout poetry if I have only ever doodled on a Post-it note?*

If you are confronting those same anxieties, I hope I can empower you with a simple truth: You own this book. Every document, every page, and every word collected here is an extension of your civic identity. These texts are an opportunity to honor, challenge, and transform the rulings, speeches, and writings that determine your political life every day.

If you are questioning how anyone could blackout such serious texts like the Declaration of Independence, the *Roe v. Wade* ruling, or the Chinese Exclusion Act, I hope I can assure you with another truth: You are owed a conversation with what rules you. When poet Niina Pollari blacks out citizenship applications to highlight harsh truths of the American immigration process, she is worthy of that conversation. When writer jayy dodd erases parts of the inaugural poem to expose a hypocritical and disconnected president, they are worthy of that conversation. When you pick up a Sharpie, a paintbrush or a pair of craft scissors to reshape these ordinances, addresses, and government records, you are worthy of that conversation.

If you are unsure of what your place is within the hierarchy and mechanisms of this political system, I implore you to go digging through these pages. Every word you black out in this book brings you closer to the truths of your American identity. Every line you scribble over, every sentence you cover in glitter, every paragraph you slice out with an X-Acto knife brings you closer. And whatever remains when you've finished, that is the precious distillation of what America means to you.

If this book feels small and fragile against the immense weight of lobbyists, politicians, and all manner of current governing bodies, I want you to know that blackout poetry is always a creative act of bravery. There is nothing small about painting over the Secretary of Homeland Security's memo on enforcing immigration laws. There is nothing fragile about lifting lyricism from the *Brown v. Board of Education* ruling, which struck down segregation in schools. Whether you share your finished poems with a thousand people on your social media or tuck them away under a mattress to keep for yourself, you have forged an identity—your unique identity—with American texts that, too often, exist outside of the very people they most affect.

If you are ready to draw, cut, glue, collage, smudge, scribble, or paint your way through a more personal understanding of the words that define America, then I encourage you to black them out with equal parts empathy and imagination. Let the honesty of your creative desires and the even deeper honesty of what you feel is right and compassionate inspire you to craft poems brimming with what America should be and overflowing with what America could be.

—Jerrod Schwarz

Declaration of Independence
Written June–July 1776
Ratified July 4, 1776

First annual message
Delivered by President Calvin Coolidge

Chinese Exclusion Act

Third annual message
Delivered by President Woodrow Wilson

Remarks at the signing of the Immigration and Nationality Act at Liberty Island, New York
Delivered by President Lyndon B. Johnson

Remarks by the president in address to the nation on immigration
Delivered by President Barack Obama

Memorandum
From: John Kelly, Secretary of Homeland Security
Subject: Enforcement of the Immigration Laws to Serve the National Interest

AMERICA AND CIVIL RIGHTS

Keynote speech to the Second National Negro Congress
Delivered by A. Philip Randolph

The Meaning of July Fourth for the Negro
Delivered by Frederick Douglass

Constitution of the United States

Dred Scott v. Sandford, **US Supreme Court**
Majority opinion delivered by Chief Justice Roger Taney

First annual message to Congress
Delivered by President Andrew Jackson

Dawes Act

An Indian's View of Indian Affairs
Delivered by Chief Joseph

Gettysburg Address
Delivered by President Abraham Lincoln

US Constitution, Thirteenth Amendment

US Constitution, Fourteenth Amendment

Lynch Law in All Its Phases
Delivered by Ida B. Wells

Brown v. Board of Education, **US Supreme Court**
Opinion delivered by Chief Justice Earl Warren

Special message to Congress
Delivered by President Lyndon B. Johnson

Remarks by the president on the fiftieth anniversary of the Selma to Montgomery marches
Delivered by President Barack Obama

Korematsu v. United States, **US Supreme Court**
Dissenting opinion delivered by Justice Robert Jackson

Memorandum
From: Clifford L. Stanley, Under Secretary of Defense
Subject: Repeal of "Don't Ask, Don't Tell"

Obergefell v. Hodges, **US Supreme Court**
Majority opinion delivered by Justice Anthony M. Kennedy

AMERICAN WOMEN

Ruth Bader Ginsburg, in an interview with *USA Today*

Letter from Abigail Adams to John Adams

Remarks to the Committee of the Judiciary of the United States Congress
Delivered by Elizabeth Cady Stanton

Nineteenth Amendment

Remarks to the Senate
Delivered by Rebecca Latimer Felton

Equal Rights Amendment

Title IX of the Education Amendments of 1972
Chapter 38, Sec. 1681. Sex

Roe v. Wade, **US Supreme Court**
Majority opinion delivered by Justice Harry A. Blackmun

House Resolution 4155
Congressional Sexual Harassment Training Act

AMERICA AND THE LAND

"America the Beautiful"
By Katharine Lee Bates

Homestead Act

The Frontier in American History
By Frederick Jackson Turner

Antiquities Act of 1906

Remarks on Antiquities Act designations
Delivered by President Donald J. Trump

Keynote address to the 1908 Conference of Governors
Delivered by President Theodore Roosevelt

Special Message to the Congress about Reorganization Plans to Establish the Environmental Protection Agency and the National Oceanic and Atmospheric Administration
Delivered by President Richard Nixon

Remarks at the Kyoto Climate Change Conference
Delivered by Vice President Al Gore

Climate Science Special Report: Fourth National Climate Assessment, **Volume I**
By the US Global Change Research Program, Washington, DC

BEGINNINGS

here

sir,

The

people

govern.

"Give Me Liberty Or Give Me Death"
By PATRICK HENRY
March 23, 1775

HOMEWORK:

Write a short essay contextualizing Patrick Henry's speech to the
Second Virginia Convention. Identify what events led him to call
for war with Britain and make his now famous declaration to "give
me liberty or give me death."

They tell us, sir, that we are weak; unable to cope with so
formidable an adversary. But when shall we be stronger? Will it
be the next week, or the next year? Will it be when we are totally
disarmed, and when a British guard shall be stationed in every
house? Shall we gather strength by irresolution and inaction?
Shall we acquire the means of effectual resistance by lying supinely
on our backs and hugging the delusive phantom of hope, until our
enemies shall have bound us hand and foot? Sir, we are not weak
if we make a proper use of those means which the God of nature hath
placed in our power. The millions of people, armed in the holy
cause of liberty, and in such a country as that which we possess,
are invincible by any force which our enemy can send against us.
Besides, sir, we shall not fight our battles alone. There is a
just God who presides over the destinies of nations, and who will
raise up friends to fight our battles for us. The battle, sir,
is not to the strong alone; it is to the vigilant, the active,
the brave. Besides, sir, we have no election. If we were base enough
to desire it, it is now too late to retire from the contest. There
is no retreat but in submission and slavery! Our chains are forged!
Their clanking may be heard on the plains of Boston! The war is
inevitable-and let it come! I repeat it, sir, let it come.

It is in vain, sir, to extenuate the matter. Gentlemen may cry,
Peace, Peace-but there is no peace. The war is actually begun!
The next gale that sweeps from the north will bring to our ears
the clash of resounding arms! Our brethren are already in the field!
Why stand we here idle? What is it that gentlemen wish? What would
they have? Is life so dear, or peace so sweet, as to be purchased
at the price of chains and slavery? Forbid it, Almighty God! I
know not what course others may take; but as for me, give me
liberty or give me death!

Declaration of Independence
Written June–July 1776
Ratified July 4, 1776

THE UNANIMOUS
DECLARATION
OF THE **THIRTEEN**
UNITED STATES OF AMERICA,

When in the Course of human events, it becomes necessary for one people to dissolve the political bands which have connected them with another, and to assume among the powers of the earth, the separate and equal station to which the Laws of Nature and of Nature's God entitle them, a decent respect to the opinions of mankind requires that they should declare the causes which impel them to the separation.

We hold these truths to be self-evident, that all men are created equal, that they are endowed by their Creator with certain unalienable Rights, that among these are Life, Liberty and the pursuit of Happiness.—That to secure these rights, Governments are instituted among Men, deriving their just powers from the consent of the governed,—That whenever any Form of Government becomes destructive of these ends, it is the Right of the People to alter or to abolish it, and to institute new Government, laying its foundation on such principles and organizing its powers in such form, as to them shall seem most likely to effect their Safety and Happiness. Prudence, indeed, will dictate that Governments long established should not be changed for light and transient causes; and accordingly all experience hath shewn, that mankind are more disposed to suffer, while evils are sufferable, than to right themselves by abolishing the forms to which they are accustomed. But when a long train of abuses and usurpations, pursuing invariably the same Object evinces a design to reduce them under absolute Despotism,

The Federalist Papers: No. 51
By ALEXANDER HAMILTON or
JAMES MADISON · February 8, 1788

NUMBER LI.

In the constitution of the judiciary department in particular, it might be inexpedient to insist rigorously on the principle: first, because peculiar qualifications being essential in the members, the primary consideration ought to be to select that mode of choice which best secures these qualifications; secondly, because the permanent tenure by which the appointments are held in that department, must soon destroy all sense of dependence on the authority conferring them.

It is equally evident, that the members of each department should be a little dependent as possible on those of the others, for the emoluments annexed to their offices. Were the executive magistrate, or the judges, not independent of the legislature in this particular, their independence in every other would be merely nominal. But the great security against a gradual concentration of the several powers in the same department, consists in giving to those who administer each department the necessary constitutional means and personal motives to resist encroachments of the others. The provision for defense must in this, as in all other cases, be made commensurate to the danger of attack. Ambition must be made to counteract ambition. The interest of the man must be connected with the constitutional rights of the place. It may be a reflection on human nature, that such devices should be necessary to control the abuses of government. But what is government itself, but the greatest of all reflections on human nature? If men were angels, no government would be necessary. If angels were to govern men, neither external nor internal controls on government would be necessary. In framing a government which is to be administered by men over men, the great difficulty lies in this: you must first enable the government to control the governed; and in the next place oblige it to control itself.

A dependence on the people is, no doubt, the primary control on the government; but experience has taught mankind the necessity of auxiliary precautions. This policy of supplying, by opposite and rival interests, the defect of better motives, might be traced through the whole system of human affairs, private as well as public. We see it particularly displayed in all the subordinate distributions of power, where the constant aim is to divide and arrange the several offices in such a manner as that each may be a check on the other that the private interest of every individual may be a sentinel over the public rights.

Washington's Farewell Address
By GEORGE WASHINGTON
September 19, 1796

BUT the Constitution which at any time exists, till changed by an explicit and authentic act of the whole people, is sacredly obligatory upon all. The very idea of the power and the right of the people to establish government presupposes the duty of every individual to obey the established government.

All obstructions to the execution of the laws, all combinations and associations, under whatever plausible character, with the real design to direct, control, counteract, or awe the regular deliberation and action of the constituted authorities, are destructive of this fundamental principle, and of fatal tendency. They serve to organize faction, to give it an artificial and extraordinary force; to put, in the place of the delegated will of the nation the will of a party, often a small but artful and enterprising minority of the community; and, according to the alternate triumphs of different parties, to make the public administration the mirror of the ill-concerted and incongruous projects of faction, rather than the organ of consistent and wholesome plans digested by common counsels and modified by mutual interests.

However combinations or associations of the above description may now and then answer popular ends, they are likely, in the course of time and things, to become potent engines, by which cunning, ambitious, and unprincipled men will be enabled to subvert the power of the people and to usurp for themselves the reins of government, destroying afterwards the very engines which have lifted them to unjust dominion.

Towards the preservation of your government, and the permanency of your present happy state, it is requisite, not only that you steadily discountenance irregular oppositions to its acknowledged authority, but also that you resist with care the spirit of innovation upon its principles, however specious the pretexts. One method of assault may be to effect, in the forms of the Constitution,

The Federalist Papers: No. 10
By JAMES MADISON
November 23, 1787

NATION VS. STATE
STRIKING A BALANCE

In this tenth essay from *The Federalist Papers*, author James Madison praises the newly minted federal Constitution for securing representation of its citizens on both the State and national levels. State electors safeguard the more particular interests of their communities, while voters on the national level attend to the interests of the country as a whole.

In the first place, it is to be remarked that, however small the republic may be, the representatives must be raised to a certain number, in order to guard against the cabals of a few; and that, however large it may be, they must be limited to a certain number, in order to guard against the confusion of a multitude. Hence, the number of representatives in the two cases not being in proportion to that of the two constituents, and being proportionally greater in the small republic, it follows that, if the

proportion of fit characters be not less in the large than in the small republic, the former will present a greater option, and consequently a greater probability of a fit choice.

In the next place, as each representative will be chosen by a greater number of citizens in the large than in the small republic, it will be more difficult for unworthy candidates to practice with success the vicious arts by which elections are too often carried; and the suffrages of the people being more free, will be more likely to centre in men who possess the most attractive merit and the most diffusive and established characters.

It must be confessed that in this, as in most other cases, there is a mean, on both sides of which inconveniences will be found to lie. By enlarging too much the number of electors, you render the representatives too little acquainted with all their local circumstances and lesser interests; as by reducing it too much, you render him unduly attached to these, and too little fit to comprehend and pursue great and national objects. The federal Constitution forms a happy combination in this respect; the great and aggregate interests being referred to the national, the local and particular to the State legislatures.

Cato: No. 3
By CATO (likely GEORGE CLINTON)
Fall 1787

CATO

NO. 3   FALL 1787

The recital, or premises on which this new form of government is erected, declares a consolidation or union of all the thirteen parts, or states, into one great whole, under the firm [form?] of the United States, for all the various and important purposes therein set forth. — But whoever seriously considers the immense extent of territory comprehended within the limits of the United States, together with the variety of its climates, productions, and commerce, the difference of extent, and number of inhabitants in all; the dissimilitude of interest, morals, and policies, in almost every one, will receive it as an intuitive truth, that a consolidated republican form of government therein, can never *form a perfect union, establish justice, insure domestic tranquility, promote the general welfare, and secure the blessings of liberty to you and your posterity,* for to these objects it must be directed: this unkindred legislature therefore, composed of interests opposite and dissimilar in their nature, will in its exercise, emphatically be, like a house divided against itself.

The governments of Europe have taken their limits and form from adventitious circumstances, and nothing can be argued on the motive of agreement from them; but these adventitious political principles, have nevertheless produced effects that have attracted the attention of philosophy, which has established axioms in the science of politics therefrom, as irrefragable as any in Euclid. It is natural, says Montesquieu, *to a republic to have only a small territory, otherwise it cannot long subsist: in a large one, there are men of large fortunes, and consequently of less moderation; there are too great deposits to intrust in the hands of a single subject, an ambitious person soon becomes sensible that he may be happy, great, and glorious by oppressing his fellow citizens, and that he might raise himself to grandeur, on the ruins of his country. In large republics, the public good is sacrificed to a thousand views; in a small one the interest of the public is easily perceived, better understood, and more within the reach of*

Constitution of the United States
Written September 17, 1787
Ratified March 4, 1789

THE
CONSTITUTION
OF THE
UNITED STATES.

W E THE PEOPLE OF THE UNITED STATES, in Order to form a more perfect Union, establish Justice, insure domestic Tranquility, provide for the common defence, promote the general Welfare, and secure the Blessings of Liberty to ourselves and our Posterity, do ordain and establish this Constitution for the United States of America.

ARTICLE. I.

SECTION 1. All legislative Powers herein granted shall be vested in a Congress of the United States, which shall consist of a Senate and House of Representatives.

SECTION 2. The House of Representatives shall be composed of Members chosen every second Year by the People of the several States, and the Electors in each State shall have the Qualifications requisite for Electors of the most numerous Branch of the State Legislature.

No Person shall be a Representative who shall not have attained to the Age of twenty five Years, and been seven

See It Now

"A Report on Senator Joseph R. McCarthy"

By EDWARD R. MURROW · CBS

March 9, 1954

EXPRESSION IN AMERICA

confuse

dissent,

with

We

must

not a

disloyalty,

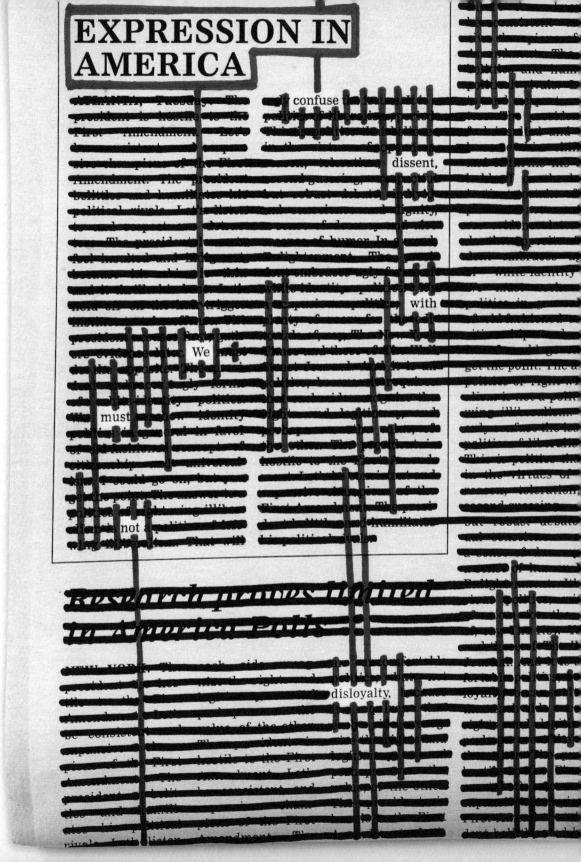

Silence Dogood Letter: No. 8
By SILENCE DOGOOD
(BENJAMIN FRANKLIN)
Published in the *New England Courant*
July 9, 1722

THE
New-England C

From MONDAY July 2. to MONDAY

To the Author of the New-England Courant.

SIR,

PREFER the following Abstract from the London Journal to any Thing of my own, and therefore shall present it to your Readers this week without any further Preface.

"WITHOUT Freedom of Thought, there can be no such Thing as Wisdom; and no such Thing as publick Liberty, without Freedom of Speech; which is the Right of every Man, as far as by it, he does not hurt or controul the Right of another: And this is the only Check it ought to suffer, and the only Bounds it ought to know.

" This sacred Privilege is so essential to free Governments, that the Security of Property, and the Freedom of Speech always go together; and in those wretched Countries where a Man cannot call his Tongue his own, he can scarce call any Thing else his own. Whoever would overthrow the Liberty of a Nation, must begin by subduing the Freeness of Speech; a Thing terrible to Publick Traytors.

" This Secret was so well known to the Court of

King Charles the Firs
procured a Proclamati
talk of Parliaments, w
aside. To assert the ur
ject, and defend his M
called Disaffection, an
People were forbid to t
ilies: For the Priests h
isters to cook up Tyra
the Law, while the la
of York, went avowedl
imprisoned and undon
And that King Charles
securely a Papist, ther
made, declaring it Trea

" That Men ought to
nours is true, while the
well spoken of; but to
hearing of it, is only th
Tyranny: A free Peop
are so, by their Freedo

" The Administratio
ing else but the Atten
People upon the Intere
And as it is the Part
whose Sake alone all p

The Bill of Rights
Passed by CONGRESS
September 25, 1789
Ratified December 15, 1791

I n response to concerns about safeguarding individual rights, several amendments were proposed to more fully articulate the personal freedoms guaranteed to citizens by the government. What follows is a transcript of these first ten amendments, collectively known as the Bill of Rights.

CONGRESS OF THE UNITED STATES BEGUN AND HELD AT THE CITY OF NEW-YORK, ON WEDNESDAY THE FOURTH OF MARCH, ONE THOUSAND SEVEN HUNDRED AND EIGHTY NINE.

THE Conventions of a number of the States, having at the time of their adopting the Constitution, expressed a desire, in order to prevent misconstruction or abuse of its powers, that further declaratory and restrictive clauses should be added: And as extending the ground of public confidence in the Government, will best ensure the beneficent ends of its institution.

RESOLVED by the Senate and House of Representatives of the United States of America, in Congress assembled, two thirds of both Houses concurring, that the following Articles be proposed to the Legislatures of the several States, as amendments to the Constitution of the United States, all, or any of which Articles, when ratified by three fourths of the said Legislatures, to be valid to all intents and purposes, as part of the said Constitution; viz.

ARTICLES in addition to, and Amendment of the Constitution of the United States of America, proposed by Congress, and ratified by the Legislatures of the several States, pursuant to the fifth Article of the original Constitution.

AMENDMENT I

Congress shall make no law respecting an establishment of religion, or prohibiting the free exercise thereof; or abridging the freedom of speech, or of the press; or the right of the people peaceably to assemble, and to petition the Government for a redress of grievances.

AMENDMENT II

A well regulated Militia, being necessary to the security of a free State, the right of the people to keep and bear Arms, shall not be infringed.

Free Speech in Wartime
Delivered by ROBERT M. LA
FOLLETTE, SR. to the Senate
October 6, 1917

He must be most
ient of the military
ust beware of those
itrary action by ad-
excused on the plea
come the fixed rule
sed and normal con-

and his representa-
war must maintain
ore than in times of
he channels for free
mental policies shall
lieve, Mr. President,
on the most impor-
y today—and that is
of this country and
ngress to discuss in
publicly and with-
m and through the
ase of this war; its
h it should be con-
which peace should
is becoming wide-
s most fundamental
the citizens of this
dous significance of
ave not yet begun to
, Mr. President, for
ht of the sovereign
make their voice
e heeded upon the
of this war, includ-
shall be prosecuted
ich it may be termi-
r the rights and the
d the interests of

right because the ex-

tremists that they monopolize the right of public utterance upon these questions unchallenged, what think you would be the consequences to this country not only during the war but after the war?

RIGHT OF PEOPLE TO DISCUSS WAR ISSUES [3]

Mr. President, our government, above all others, is founded on the right of the people freely to discuss all matters pertaining to their government, in war not less than in peace, for in this government the people are the rulers in war no less than in peace. It is true, sir, that members of the House of Representatives are elected for two years, the president for four years, and the members of the Senate for six years, and during their temporary official terms these officers constitute what is called the government. But back of them always is the controlling sovereign power of the people, and when the people can make their will known, the faithful officer will obey that will. Though the right of the people to express their will by ballot is suspended during the term of office of the elected official, nevertheless the duty of the official to obey the popular will continues throughout his entire term of office. How can that popular will express itself between elections except by meetings, by speeches, by publications, by petitions, and by addresses to the representatives of the people? Any man who seeks to set a limit upon those rights, whether in war or peace, aims a blow at the most vital part of our government. And then as the time for election approaches and the official is called to account for his stewardship—not a day, not a week, not a month, before the election, but a year or more before it, if the people choose— they must have the right to the freest possible

New York Times Co. v. United States, **US Supreme Court**
Majority opinion delivered by
JUSTICE HUGO BLACK
June 30, 1971

that they were, wrote in language they earnestly believed could never be misunderstood: "Congress shall make no law . . . abridging the freedom . . . of the press. . . ." Both the history and language of the First Amendment support the view that the press must be left free to publish news, whatever the source, without censorship, injunctions, or prior restraints.

In the First Amendment, the Founding Fathers gave the free press the protection it must have to fulfill its essential role in our democracy. The press was to serve the governed, not the governors. The Government's power to censor the press was abolished so that the press would remain forever free to censure the Government. The press was protected so that it could bare the secrets of government and inform the people. Only a free and unrestrained press can effectively expose deception in government. And paramount among the responsibilities of a free press is the duty to prevent any part of the government from deceiving the people and sending them off to distant lands to die of foreign fevers and foreign shot and shell. In my view, far from deserving condemnation for their courageous reporting, the New York Times, the Washington Post, and other newspapers should be commended for serving the purpose that the Founding Fathers saw so clearly. In revealing the workings of government that led to the Vietnam war, the newspapers nobly did precisely that which the Founders hoped and trusted they would do.

The Government's case here is based on premises entirely different from those that guided the Framers of the First Amendment. The Solicitor General has carefully and emphatically stated:

"Now, Mr. Justice [BLACK], your construction of . . . [the First Amendment] is well known, and I certainly respect it. You say that no law means no

Memorandum for All Executive Departments and Agencies
From: THE ATTORNEY GENERAL, JEFF SESSIONS
Subject: Federal Law Protections for Religious Liberty
October 6, 2017

Office of the Attorney General

Washington, D.C. 20530

October 6, 2017

MEMORANDUM FOR ALL EXECUTIVE DEPARTMENTS AND AGENCIES

FROM: THE ATTORNEY GENERAL

SUBJECT: <u>Federal Law Protections for Religious Liberty</u>

        The President has instructed me to issue guidance interpreting religious liberty protections in federal law, as appropriate. Exec. Order No. 13798 § 4, 82 Fed. Reg. 21675 (May 4, 2017). Consistent with that instruction, I am issuing this memorandum and appendix to guide all administrative agencies and executive departments in the execution of federal law.

Principles of Religious Liberty

        Religious liberty is a foundational principle of enduring importance in America, enshrined in our Constitution and other sources of federal law. As James Madison explained in his Memorial and Remonstrance Against Religious Assessments, the free exercise of religion "is in its nature an unalienable right" because the duty owed to one's Creator "is precedent, both in order of time and in degree of obligation, to the claims of Civil Society."[1] Religious liberty is not merely a right to personal religious beliefs or even to worship in a sacred place. It also encompasses religious observance and practice. Except in the narrowest circumstances, no one should be forced to choose between living out his or her faith and complying with the law. Therefore, to the greatest extent practicable and permitted by law, religious observance and practice should be reasonably accommodated in all government activity, including employment, contracting, and programming. The following twenty principles should guide administrative agencies and executive departments in carrying out this task. These principles should be understood and interpreted in light of the legal analysis set forth in the appendix to this memorandum.

1. **The freedom of religion is a fundamental right of paramount importance, expressly protected by federal law.**

        Religious liberty is enshrined in the text of our Constitution and in numerous federal statutes. It encompasses the right of all Americans to exercise their religion freely, without being coerced to join an established church or to satisfy a religious test as a qualification for public office. It also encompasses the right of all Americans to express their religious beliefs, subject to the same narrow limits that apply to all forms of speech. In the United States, the free exercise of religion is not a mere policy preference to be traded against other policy preferences. It is a fundamental right.

---

[1] James Madison, Memorial and Remonstrance Against Religious Assessments (June 20, 1785), *in* 5 THE FOUNDERS' CONSTITUTION 82 (Philip B. Kurland & Ralph Lerner eds., 1987).

**A Bill for Establishing
Religious Freedom**
By THOMAS JEFFERSON
June 18, 1779

hing RELIGIOUS FREEDOM,

onfederation of the PEOPLE.

THAT the impious presumption of legislators and rulers, civil as well as ecclesiastical, who, being themselves but fallible and uninspired men have assumed dominion over the faith of others, setting up their own opinions and modes of thinking as the only true and infallible, and as such endeavouring to impose them on others, hath established and maintained false religions over the greatest part of the world and through all time;

THAT to compel a man to furnish contributions of money for the propagation of opinions, which he disbelieves is sinful and tyrannical;

THAT even the forcing him to support this or that teacher of his own religious persuasion is depriving him of the comfortable liberty of giving his contributions to the particular pastor, whose morals he would make his pattern, and whose powers he feels most persuasive to righteousness, and is withdrawing from the Ministry those temporary rewards, which, proceeding from an approbation of their personal conduct are an additional incitement to earnest and unremitting labours for the instruction of mankind;

THAT our civil rights have no dependence on our religious opinions any more than our opinions in physics or geometry,

THAT therefore the proscribing any citizen as unworthy the public confidence, by laying upon him an incapacity of being called to offices of trust and emolument, unless he profess or renounce this or that religious opinion, is depriving him injuriously of those privileges and advantages, to which, in common with his fellow citizens, he has a natural right,

THAT it tends only to corrupt the principles of that very Religion it is meant to encourage, by bribing with a monopoly of worldly honours and

**Remarks at the Islamic Center
of Washington, DC**
Delivered by PRESIDENT GEORGE W.
BUSH · September 17, 2001

THE WHITE HOUSE
PRESIDENT
GEORGE W. BUSH

 CLICK HERE TO PRINT

For Immediate Release
Office of the Press Secretary
September 17, 2001

"Islam is Peace" Says President
Remarks by the President at Islamic Center of Washington, D.C.
Washington, D.C.

View the President's Remarks
Listen to the President's Remarks

3:12 P.M. EDT

THE PRESIDENT: Thank you all very much for your hospitality. We've just had a—wide-ranging discussions on the matter at hand. Like the good folks standing with me, the American people were appalled and outraged at last Tuesday's attacks. And so were Muslims all across the world. Both Americans and Muslim friends and citizens, tax-paying citizens, and Muslims in nations were just appalled and could not believe what we saw on our TV screens.

These acts of violence against innocents violate the fundamental tenets of the Islamic faith. And it's important for my fellow Americans to understand that.

The English translation is not as eloquent as the original Arabic, but let me quote from the Koran, itself: In the long run, evil in the extreme will be the end of those who do evil. For that they rejected the signs of Allah and held them up to ridicule.

The face of terror is not the true faith of Islam. That's not what Islam is all about. Islam is peace. These terrorists don't represent peace. They represent evil and war.

When we think of Islam we think of a faith that brings comfort to a billion people around the world. Billions of people find comfort and solace and peace. And that's made brothers and sisters out of every race—out of every race.

America counts millions of Muslims amongst our citizens, and Muslims make an incredibly valuable contribution to our country. Muslims are doctors, lawyers, law professors, members of the military, entrepreneurs, shopkeepers, moms and dads. And they need to be treated with respect. In our anger and emotion, our fellow Americans must treat each other with respect.

Women who cover their heads in this country must feel comfortable going outside their homes. Moms who wear cover must be not intimidated in America. That's not the America I know. That's not the America I value.

I've been told that some fear to leave; some don't want to go shopping for their families; some don't want to go about their ordinary daily routines because, by wearing cover, they're afraid they'll be intimidated. That should not and that will not stand in America.

Those who feel like they can intimidate our fellow citizens to take out their anger don't represent the best of America, they represent the worst of humankind, and they should be ashamed of that kind of behavior.

This is a great country. It's a great country because we share the same values of respect and dignity and human worth. And it is my honor to be meeting with leaders who feel just the same way I do. They're outraged, they're sad. They love America just as much as I do.

I want to thank you all for giving me a chance to come by. And may God bless us all.

END   3:19 P.M. EDT

**Presidential proclamation—
Religious Freedom Day, 2017**
By PRESIDENT BARACK OBAMA
January 13, 2017

For Immediate Release   January 13, 2017

Presidential Proclamation — Religious Freedom Day, 2017

RELIGIOUS FREEDOM DAY, 2017
- - - - - - -
BY THE PRESIDENT OF THE UNITED STATES OF AMERICA

A PROCLAMATION

Believing that "Almighty God hath created the mind free," Thomas Jefferson authored
the Virginia Statute for Religious Freedom after our young Nation declared its
independence. This idea of religious liberty later became a foundation for the First
Amendment, which begins by stating that "Congress shall make no law respecting an
establishment of religion, or prohibiting the free exercise thereof . . ." On Religious
Freedom Day, we rededicate ourselves to defending these fundamental principles,
pay tribute to the many ways women and men of different religious and non-religious
backgrounds have shaped America's narrative, and resolve to continue forging a future
in which all people are able to practice their faiths freely or not practice at all.

Religious freedom is a principle based not on shared ancestry, culture, ethnicity, or faith
but on a shared commitment to liberty—and it lies at the very heart of who we are as
Americans. As a Nation, our strength comes from our diversity, and we must be unified
in our commitment to protecting the freedoms of conscience and religious belief and
the freedom to live our lives according to them. Religious freedom safeguards religion,
allowing us to flourish as one of the most religious countries on Earth, but it also
strengthens our Nation as a whole. Brave men and women of faith have challenged our
conscience and brought us closer to our founding ideals, from the abolition of slavery
to the expansion of civil rights and workers' rights. And throughout our history, faith
communities have helped uphold these values by joining in efforts to help those in

Remarks at Amherst College
Delivered by PRESIDENT JOHN F.
KENNEDY · October 26, 1963

AMHERST

The artist, however faithful to his personal vision of reality,
becomes the last champion of the individual mind and sensibility
against an intrusive society and an officious state. The great
artist is thus a solitary figure. He has, as Frost said, a lover's
quarrel with the world. In pursuing his perceptions of reality,
he must often sail against the currents of his time. This is not a
popular role. If Robert Frost was much honored in his lifetime,
it was because a good many preferred to ignore his darker truths.
Yet in retrospect, we see how the artist's fidelity has
strengthened the fibre of our national life.

If sometimes our great artists have been the most critical of our
society, it is because their sensitivity and their concern for
justice, which must motivate any true artist, makes him aware that
our Nation falls short of its highest potential. I see little of
more importance to the future of our country and our
civilization than full recognition of the place of the artist.

If art is to nourish the roots of our culture, society must set
the artist free to follow his vision wherever it takes him. We
must never forget that art is not a form of propaganda; it is a
form of truth. And as Mr. MacLeish once remarked of poets, there
is nothing worse for our trade than to be in style. In free
society art is not a weapon and it does not belong to the spheres

**20 US Code subchapter I—
National Foundation on the Arts
and the Humanities**
§ 951—Declaration of findings and
purposes · August 2010

**NATIONAL FOUNDATION ON THE ARTS AND THE HUMANITIES ACT OF 1965,
NATIONAL ENDOWMENT FOR THE ARTS FISCAL YEAR 2010 APPROPRIATIONS,
AND RELATED AGENCIES**

20 U.S.C. § 951 (2010)

§ 951. Declaration of findings and purposes

The Congress finds and declares the following:

(1)   The arts and the humanities belong to all the people of the United States.

(2)   The encouragement and support of national progress and scholarship in the humanities and the arts, while primarily a matter for private and local initiative, are also appropriate matters of concern to the Federal Government.

(3)   An advanced civilization must not limit its efforts to science and technology alone, but must give full value and support to the other great branches of scholarly and cultural activity in order to achieve a better understanding of the past, a better analysis of the present, and a better view of the future.

(4)   Democracy demands wisdom and vision in its citizens. It must therefore foster and support a form of education, and access to the arts and the humanities, designed to make people of all backgrounds and wherever located masters of their technology and not its unthinking servants.

(5)   It is necessary and appropriate for the Federal Government to complement, assist, and add to programs for the advancement of the humanities and the arts by local, State, regional, and private agencies and their organizations. In doing so, the Government must be sensitive to the nature of public sponsorship. Public funding of the arts and humanities is subject to the conditions that traditionally govern the use of public money. Such funding should contribute to public support and confidence in the use of taxpayer funds. Public funds provided by the Federal Government must ultimately serve public purposes the Congress defines.

(6)   The arts and the humanities reflect the high place accorded by the American people to the nation's rich cultural heritage and to the fostering of mutual respect for the diverse beliefs and values of all persons and groups.

(7)   The practice of art and the study of the humanities require constant dedication and devotion. While no government can call a great artist or scholar into existence, it is necessary and appropriate for the Federal Government to help create and sustain not only a climate encouraging freedom of thought, imagination, and inquiry but also the material conditions facilitating the release of this creative talent.

(8)   The world leadership which has come to the United States cannot rest solely upon superior power, wealth, and technology, but must be solidly founded upon worldwide respect and admiration for the Nation's high qualities as a leader in the realm of ideas and of the spirit.

(9)   Americans should receive in school, background and preparation in the arts and humanities to enable them to recognize and appreciate the aesthetic dimensions of our lives, the diversity of excellence that comprises our cultural heritage, and artistic and scholarly expression.

Nixon v. Shrink Missouri
Government PAC,
US Supreme Court
Concurring opinion delivered by
JUSTICE PAUL STEVENS
January 24, 2000

MONEY AND SPEECH IN POLITICAL CAMPAIGNS

In this Supreme Court case, the court ruled in favor of limiting campaign contributions on a State level, upholding the precedent established for limitations on federal campaign contributions in *Buckley v. Valeo*. Associate Justice Paul Stevens delivered a concurring opinion which distilled the court's findings into seven simple words: Money is property; it is not speech.

**JEREMIAH W. (JAY) NIXON, ATTORNEY GENERAL OF MISSOURI, et al.,
PETITIONERS v. SHRINK MISSOURI GOVERNMENT PAC et al.**

**ON WRIT OF CERTIORARI TO THE UNITED STATES COURT
OF APPEALS FOR THE EIGHTH CIRCUIT**

[January 24, 2000]

Justice Stevens, concurring.

Justice Kennedy suggests that the misuse of soft money tolerated by this Court's misguided decision in *Colorado Republican Federal Campaign Comm. v. Federal Election Comm'n*, 518 U.S. 604 (1996), demonstrates the need for a fresh examination of the constitutional issues raised by Congress' enactment of the Federal Election Campaign Acts of 1971 and 1974 and this Court's resolution of those issues in *Buckley v. Valeo*, 424 U.S. 1 (1976) (per curiam). In response to his call for a new beginning, therefore, I make one simple point. Money is property; it is not speech.

Speech has the power to inspire volunteers to perform a multitude of tasks on a campaign trail, on a battleground, or even on a football field. Money, meanwhile, has the power to pay hired laborers to perform the same tasks. It does not follow, however, that the First Amendment provides the same measure of protection to the use of money to accomplish such goals as it provides to the use of ideas to achieve the same results.

Our Constitution and our heritage properly protect the individual's interest in making decisions about the use of his or her own property. Governmental regulation of such decisions can sometimes be viewed either as "deprivations of liberty" or as "deprivations of property," see, e.g., *Moore v. East Cleveland*, 431 U.S. 494, 513 (1977) (Stevens, J., concurring in judgment). Telling a grandmother that she may not use her own property to provide shelter to a grandchild–or to

Address at the groundbreaking ceremonies for the Eisenhower Library, Abilene, Kansas
Delivered by PRESIDENT DWIGHT D. EISENHOWER · October 13, 1959

AMERICA AND THE WORLD

The world must learn to work together or finally it will not work at all

The Fourteen Points
Delivered by PRESIDENT WOODROW
WILSON in an address to Congress
January 8, 1918

The Fourteen Points

We entered this war because violations of right had occurred which touched us to the quick and made the life of our own people impossible unless they were corrected and the world secure once for all against their recurrence. What we demand in this war, therefore, is nothing peculiar to ourselves. It is that the world be made fit and safe to live in ; and particularly that it be made safe for every peace-loving nation which, like our own, wishes to live its own life, determine its own institutions, be assured of justice and fair dealing by the other peoples of the world as against force and selfish aggression. All the peoples of the world are in effect partners in this interest, and for our own part we see very clearly that unless justice be done to others it will not be done to us. The programme of the world's peace, therefore, is our programme ; and that programme, the only possible programme, as we see it, is this :

I. Open covenants of peace, openly arrived at, after which there shall be no private international understandings of any kind but diplomacy shall proceed always frankly and in the public view.

II. Absolute freedom of navigation upon the seas, outside territorial waters, alike in peace and in war, except as the seas may be closed in whole or in part by international action for the enforcement of international covenants.

III. The removal, so far as possible, of all economic barriers and the establishment of an equality of trade conditions among all the nations consenting to the peace and associating themselves for its maintenance.

IV. Adequate guarantees given and taken that national armaments will be reduced to the lowest point consistent with domestic safety.

The Marshall Plan speech
Delivered by SECRETARY OF STATE
GEORGE C. MARSHALL to the
Harvard Alumni Association
June 5, 1947

The remedy lies in breaking the vicious circle and restoring the confidence of the European people in the economic future of their own countries and of Europe as a whole. The manufacturer and the farmer throughout wide areas must be able and willing to exchange their products for currencies the continuing value of which is not open to question.

Aside from the demoralizing effect on the world at large and the possibilities of disturbances arising as a result of the desperation of the people concerned, the consequences to the economy of the United States should be apparent to all. It is logical that the United States should do whatever it is able to do to assist in the return of normal economic health in the world, without which there can be no political stability and no assured peace. Our policy is directed not against any country or doctrine but against hunger, poverty, desperation and chaos. Its purpose should be the revival of a working economy in the world so as to permit the emergence of political and social conditions in which free institutions can exist. Such assistance, I am convinced, must not be on a piece-meal basis as various crises develop. Any assistance that this Government may render in the future should provide a cure rather than a mere palliative.

Lend-Lease Act
Enacted March 11, 1941

year, the computation and information based on such credit may be omitted from the return.

"(2) No RETURN REQUIRED.—".

SEC. 17. EFFECTIVE DATE.

The amendments made by this Act shall be effective as of the date of enactment of the Excess Profits Tax Act of 1940.

Approved, March 7, 1941.

54 Stat. 975, 1018.
26 U. S. C. §§ 710–752.

[CHAPTER 11]

AN ACT

Further to promote the defense of the United States, and for other purposes.

March 11, 1941
[H. R. 1776]
[Public Law 11]

Be it enacted by the Senate and House of Representatives of the United States of America in Congress assembled, That this Act may be cited as "An Act to Promote the Defense of the United States".

An Act to Promote the Defense of the United States.
Post, p. 236.

SEC. 2. As used in this Act—

(a) The term "defense article" means—

"Defense article."

(1) Any weapon, munition, aircraft, vessel, or boat;

(2) Any machinery, facility, tool, material, or supply necessary for the manufacture, production, processing, repair, servicing, or operation of any article described in this subsection;

(3) Any component material or part of or equipment for any article described in this subsection;

(4) Any agricultural, industrial or other commodity or article for defense.

Such term "defense article" includes any article described in this subsection: Manufactured or procured pursuant to section 3, or to which the United States or any foreign government has or hereafter acquires title, possession, or control.

(b) The term "defense information" means any plan, specification, design, prototype, or information pertaining to any defense article.

"Defense information."

SEC. 3. (a) Notwithstanding the provisions of any other law, the President may, from time to time, when he deems it in the interest of national defense, authorize the Secretary of War, the Secretary of the Navy, or the head of any other department or agency of the Government—

Powers of the President.

(1) To manufacture in arsenals, factories, and shipyards under their jurisdiction, or otherwise procure, to the extent to which funds are made available therefor, or contracts are authorized from time to time by the Congress, or both, any defense article for the government of any country whose defense the President deems vital to the defense of the United States.

Manufacture, etc., of defense articles for designated governments.

(2) To sell, transfer title to, exchange, lease, lend, or otherwise dispose of, to any such government any defense article, but no defense article not manufactured or procured under paragraph (1) shall in any way be disposed of under this paragraph, except after consultation with the Chief of Staff of the Army or the Chief of Naval Operations of the Navy, or both. The value of defense articles disposed of in any way under authority of this paragraph, and procured from funds heretofore appropriated, shall not exceed $1,300,000,000. The value of such defense articles shall be determined by the head of the department or agency concerned or such other department, agency or officer as shall be designated in the manner provided in the rules and regulations issued hereunder. Defense articles procured from funds hereafter appropriated to any department or agency of the Government,

Disposal.

Limitation on value.
Post, p. 813.

Defense articles procured from future appropriations.

Statement before the fifty-fifth regular session of the UN General Assembly
Delivered by SECRETARY OF STATE
MADELEINE K. ALBRIGHT
September 12, 2000

Address by Secretary of State Madeleine K. Albright

Statement by Secretary of State Madeleine K. Albright before the 55th regular session of the UN General Assembly on September 12, 2000.

I am honored to address the Assembly on behalf of the United States and to reinforce the eloquent message President Clinton conveyed during last week's Millennium Summit. Because my father worked here when I was young, I have always considered myself a child of the United Nations. And because I had the privilege to serve here as America's Permanent Representative, I feel at home and so will speak plainly.

The members of this body reflect virtually every culture, ethnicity, and geographical region. We are city and country, inland and island, tropical and temperate, developing and industrialized. We are as diverse as humanity.

And yet, in responding to the daunting demands of this new era, we are bound together by the interests we share and the ideals to which we aspire.

We all have a stake in building peace and relieving poverty, championing development, and curbing disease. We all want to see the dangers posed by weapons of mass destruction reduced, refugees cared for, children nourished, the environment protected, and the status of women advanced.

We all believe the benefits of globalization must be allocated more broadly within and among societies. Because if the new technologies are to ease the old problems, they must help the many who today lack access and skills, so that every village becomes a home to opportunity and every school a midwife to hope.

As the Millennium Summit reflected, we have no shortage of worthy goals. We are right to aim high and take on the mightiest tasks.

But as the Secretary General has said, progress depends on working together. We need all hands on deck, pulling in the same direction. For each of us, that responsibility begins at home because the international community cannot help any nation that is not striving to help itself.

Each government has an obligation to observe international norms on human rights, uphold the rule of law, fight corruption, and raise awareness about HIV/AIDS. But in the twenty-first century, no nation can protect and serve its people simply by going it alone and that is why we all benefit from strengthening regional bodies such as the Organization of American States, the Organization of African Unity, the Association of South–East Asian Nations, and the Organization for Security and Cooperation in Europe.

Because of their unique expertise and regional legitimacy, they can be instruments for solving some of the hardest challenges we face. But they will succeed only if we raise our

The Monroe Doctrine
Delivered by PRESIDENT JAMES
MONROE in his seventh annual
message to Congress
December 2, 1823

The Monroe Doctrine

December 2, 1823

A SIMILAR PROPOSAL *has been made by His Imperial Majesty* to the Government of Great Britain, which has likewise been acceded to. The Government of the United States has been desirous by this friendly proceeding of manifesting the great value which they have invariably attached to the friendship of the Emperor and their solicitude to cultivate the best understanding with his Government. In the discussions to which this interest has given rise and in the arrangements by which they may terminate the occasion has been judged proper for asserting, as a principle in which the rights and interests of the United States are involved, that the American continents, by the free and independent condition which they have assumed and maintain, are henceforth not to be considered as subjects for future colonization by any European powers. . .

It was stated at the commencement of the last session that a great effort was then making in Spain and Portugal to improve the condition of the people of those countries, and that it appeared to be conducted with extraordinary moderation. It need scarcely be remarked that the results have been so far very different from what was then anticipated. Of events in that quarter of the globe, with which we have so much intercourse and from which we derive our origin, we have always been anxious and interested spectators. The citizens of the United States cherish sentiments the most friendly in favor of the liberty and happiness of their fellow-men on that side of the Atlantic. In the wars of the European powers in matters relating to themselves we have never taken any part, nor does it comport with our policy to do so. It is only when our rights are invaded or seriously menaced that we resent injuries or make preparation for our defense. With the movements in this hemisphere we are of necessity more immediately connected, and by causes which must be obvious to all enlightened and impartial observers. The political system of the allied powers is essentially different in this respect from that of America. This difference proceeds from that which exists in their respective Governments; and to the defense of our own, which has been achieved by the loss of so much blood and treasure, and matured by the wisdom of their most enlightened citizens, and under which we have enjoyed unexampled felicity, this whole nation is devoted. We owe it, therefore, to candor and to the amicable relations existing between the United States and those powers to declare that we should consider any attempt on their part to extend their system to any portion of this hemisphere as dangerous to our peace and safety. With the existing colonies or dependencies of any European power we have not interfered and shall not interfere. But with the Governments who have declared their independence and maintain it, and whose independence we have, on great consideration and on just principles, acknowledged, we could not view any interposition for the purpose of oppressing them, or controlling in any other manner their destiny, by any European power in any other light than as the manifestation of an unfriendly disposition toward the United States. In the war between those new Governments and Spain we declared our neutrality at

Executive Order 13228
Establishing the Office of Homeland
Security and the Homeland Security
Council · October 8, 2001

Presidential Documents

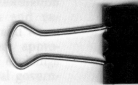

Executive Order 13228 of October 8, 2001

Establishing the Office of Homeland Security and the Homeland Security Council

By the authority vested in me as President by the Constitution and the laws of the United States of America, it is hereby ordered as follows:

Section 1. *Establishment.* I hereby establish within the Executive Office of the President an Office of Homeland Security (the "Office") to be headed by the Assistant to the President for Homeland Security.

Sec. 2. *Mission.* The mission of the Office shall be to develop and coordinate the implementation of a comprehensive national strategy to secure the United States from terrorist threats or attacks. The Office shall perform the functions necessary to carry out this mission, including the functions specified in section 3 of this order.

Sec. 3. *Functions.* The functions of the Office shall be to coordinate the executive branch's efforts to detect, prepare for, prevent, protect against, respond to, and recover from terrorist attacks within the United States.

(a) *National Strategy.* The Office shall work with executive departments and agencies, State and local governments, and private entities to ensure the adequacy of the national strategy for detecting, preparing for, preventing, protecting against, responding to, and recovering from terrorist threats or attacks within the United States and shall periodically review and coordinate revisions to that strategy as necessary.

(b) *Detection.* The Office shall identify priorities and coordinate efforts for collection and analysis of information within the United States regarding threats of terrorism against the United States and activities of terrorists or terrorist groups within the United States. The Office also shall identify, in coordination with the Assistant to the President for National Security Affairs, priorities for collection of intelligence outside the United States regarding threats of terrorism within the United States.

(i) In performing these functions, the Office shall work with Federal, State, and local agencies, as appropriate, to:

(A) facilitate collection from State and local governments and private entities of information pertaining to terrorist threats or activities within the United States;

(B) coordinate and prioritize the requirements for foreign intelligence relating to terrorism within the United States of executive departments and agencies responsible for homeland security and provide these requirements and priorities to the Director of Central Intelligence and other agencies responsible for collection of foreign intelligence;

(C) coordinate efforts to ensure that all executive departments and agencies that have intelligence collection responsibilities have sufficient technological capabilities and resources to

**Letter to Charles Erwin Wilson,
Secretary of Defense**
By ALLEN W. DULLES, CIA Director
January 29, 1955

CENTRAL INTELLIGENCE AGENCY

WASHINGTON 25, D. C.

OFFICE OF THE DIRECTOR

29 January 1955

The Honorable
The Secretary of Defense
Department of Defense
Washington 25, D. C.

Dear Mr. Secretary:

I have been following with great interest the progress in the development of the earth satellite vehicle plans. I should like to state the concern of this Agency with both the first launching of the earth satellite and its possible use in advanced form to collect intelligence data.

In addition to the cogent scientific arguments advanced in support of the development of earth satellites, there is little doubt but what the nation that first successfully launches the earth satellite, and thereby introduces the age of space travel, will gain incalculable international prestige and recognition. In many respects it will be comparable to the first release of nuclear energy. Our scientific community as well as the nation would gain invaluable respect and confidence should our country be the first to launch the satellite. Consequently, I feel the psychological impact of this development on friendly, neutral and Communist-controlled countries, particularly when we are anticipating a prolonged state of cold war, is one of the major arguments justifying its prompt development.

I should be happy to discuss the matter further at your convenience and to give any support the Agency might be able to provide in evaluating earth satellite plans. Because of the international and diplomatic implications of this project, I am sending this information to the Secretary of State.

Sincerely yours,

Allen W. Dulles
Director

CIA

SecDef Cont. No. 01399

3683

SECRET

Inaugural address
Delivered by PRESIDENT HARRY S.
TRUMAN · January 20, 1949

Suggestions / — Inaugural PRESIDENT HARRY S. TRUMAN
JANUARY 20, 1949

In the pursuit of these aims, the United States and other like-minded nations find themselves directly opposed by a regime with contrary aims and a totally different concept of life.

THAT regime adheres to a false philosophy which purports to offer freedom, security, and greater opportunity to mankind. Misled by that philosophy, many peoples have sacrificed their liberties only to learn to their sorrow that deceit and mockery, poverty and tyranny, are their reward.

THAT false philosophy is communism.

COMMUNISM is based on the belief that man is so weak and inadequate that he is unable to govern himself, and therefore requires the rule of strong masters.

DEMOCRACY is based on the conviction that man has the moral and intellectual capacity, as well as the inalienable right, to govern himself with reason and justice.

COMMUNISM subjects the individual to arrest without lawful cause, punishment without trial, and forced labor as the chattel of the state. It decrees what information he shall receive, what art he shall produce, what leaders he shall follow, and what thoughts he shall think.

DEMOCRACY maintains that government is established for the benefit of the individual, and is charged with the responsibility of protecting the rights of the individual and his freedom in the exercise of those abilities of his.

COMMUNISM maintains that social wrongs can be corrected only by violence.

DEMOCRACY has proved that social justice can be achieved through peaceful change.

COMMUNISM holds that the world is so widely divided into opposing classes that war is inevitable.

DEMOCRACY holds that free nations can settle differences justly and maintain a lasting peace.

These differences between communism and democracy do not concern the United States alone. People everywhere are coming to realize that what is involved is material well-being, human dignity, and the right to believe in and worship God.

**Remarks on East-West
relations at the Brandenburg
Gate in West Berlin**
Delivered by PRESIDENT RONALD
REAGAN · June 12, 1987

STRENGTHEN THE SOVIET SYSTEM WITHOUT CHANGING
IT? WE WELCOME CHANGE AND OPENNESS; FOR WE
BELIEVE THAT FREEDOM AND SECURITY GO TOGETHER,
THAT THE ADVANCE OF HUMAN LIBERTY CAN ONLY
STRENGTHEN THE CAUSE OF WORLD PEACE.

THERE IS ONE SIGN THE SOVIETS CAN MAKE THAT
WOULD BE UNMISTAKABLE,/THAT WOULD ADVANCE
DRAMATICALLY THE CAUSE OF FREEDOM AND PEACE.
GENERAL SECRETARY GORBACHEV, IF YOU SEEK PEACE,
IF YOU SEEK PROSPERITY FOR THE SOVIET UNION AND
EASTERN EUROPE, IF YOU SEEK LIBERALIZATION:/COME
HERE TO THIS GATE! MR. GORBACHEV, OPEN THIS
GATE! MR. GORBACHEV, TEAR DOWN THIS WALL!

I UNDERSTAND THE FEAR OF WAR AND THE PAIN OF
DIVISION THAT AFFLICT THIS CONTINENT -- AND I
PLEDGE TO YOU MY COUNTRY'S EFFORTS TO HELP
OVERCOME THESE BURDENS./TO BE SURE, WE IN THE
WEST MUST RESIST SOVIET EXPANSION. SO WE MUST

**Memorandum on reactions to a
US course of action in Vietnam**
By SENIOR OFFICERS of State/INR,
DIA, and CIA · April 21, 1965

21 April 1965

MEMORANDUM (Revised Text)

THE PROBLEM

To estimate Communist and general world reactions to a US course of action in Vietnam, stated below, over the next six to twelve months.

ASSUMPTIONS

We assume that the scale and tempo of US air action against North Vietnam and against the Viet Cong in South Vietnam continues at present levels for the period of this estimate. We also assume that, within the next few months, additional US military forces are introduced into South Vietnam to bring the total US military present there to approximately 80,000 and that these forces will have, as part of their mission, ground combat against Viet Cong troops.. We also assume that approximately 5,250 Allied non-US combat forces are introduced.

DISCUSSION

I. INTRODUCTION

1. The Present Situation. At present it appears that the DRV, with strong Chinese encouragement, is determined for the present to ride out the US bombardment. The Viet Cong, the DRV, and Communist

GROUP
Excluded from automatic
downgrading and
declassification

T-O-P S-E-C-R-E-T

**"Declarations of War
and Authorizations for the
Use of Military Force:
Historical Background and
Legal Implications"**
By the CONGRESSIONAL RESEARCH
SERVICE · April 18, 2014

Summary

From the Washington Administration to the present, Congress and the President have enacted 11 separate formal declarations of war against foreign nations in five different wars. Each declaration has been preceded by a presidential request either in writing or in person before a joint session of Congress. The reasons cited in justification for the requests have included armed attacks on United States territory or its citizens and threats to United States rights or interests as a sovereign nation.

Congress and the President have also enacted authorizations for the use of force rather than formal declarations of war. Such measures have generally authorized the use of force against either a named country or unnamed hostile nations in a given region. In most cases, the President has requested the authority, but Congress has sometimes given the President less than what he asked for. Not all authorizations for the use of force have resulted in actual combat. Both declarations and authorizations require the signature of the President in order to become law.

In contrast to an authorization, a declaration of war in itself creates a state of war under international law and legitimates the killing of enemy combatants, the seizure of enemy property, and the apprehension of enemy aliens. While a formal declaration was once deemed a necessary legal prerequisite to war and was thought to terminate diplomatic and commercial relations and most treaties between the combatants, declarations have fallen into disuse since World War II. The laws of war, such as the Hague and Geneva Conventions, apply to circumstances of armed conflict whether or not a formal declaration or authorization was issued.

With respect to domestic law, a declaration of war automatically triggers many standby statutory authorities conferring special powers on the President with respect to the military, foreign trade, transportation, communications, manufacturing, alien enemies, etc. In contrast, no standby authorities appear to be triggered automatically by an authorization for the use of force, although the executive branch has argued, with varying success, that the authorization to use force in response to the terrorist attacks of 2001 provided a statutory exception to certain statutory prohibitions.

Most statutory standby authorities do not expressly require a declaration of war to be actualized but can be triggered by a declaration of national emergency or simply by the existence of a state of war; however, courts have sometimes construed the word "war" in a statute as implying a formal declaration, leading Congress to enact clarifying amendments in two cases. Declarations of war and authorizations for the use of force waive the time limitations otherwise applicable to the use of force imposed by the War Powers Resolution.

This report provides historical background on the enactment of declarations of war and authorizations for the use of force and analyzes their legal effects under international and domestic law. It also sets forth their texts in two appendices. The report includes an extensive listing and summary of statutes that are triggered by a declaration of war, a declaration of national emergency, and/or the existence of a state of war. The report concludes with a summary of the congressional procedures applicable to the enactment of a declaration of war or authorization for the use of force and to measures under the War Powers Resolution. The report will be updated as circumstances warrant.

Memorandum for DoD
From: PATRICK M. SHANAHAN,
Deputy Secretary of Defense
Subject: Guidance for Continuation
of Operations During a Lapse of
Appropriations · January 18, 2018

MEMORANDUM FO

or the protection of property (a copy of military operations necessary for national security will be supplied separately). These activities will be "excepted" from the effects of a lapse in appropriations: all other activities would need to be shut down in an orderly and deliberate fashion, including – with few exceptions – the cessation of temporary duty travel.

All military personnel performing active duty will continue in a normal duty status regardless of their affiliation with excepted or non-excepted activities. Military personnel will not be paid until such time as Congress makes appropriated funds available to compensate them for this period of service. Civilian personnel who are necessary to carry out or support excepted activities will also continue in normal duty status and also will not be paid until Congress makes appropriated funds available. Civilian employees paid from lapsed appropriations and who are not necessary to carry out or support excepted activities will be furloughed, i.e., placed in a non-work, non-pay status.

The responsibility for determining which activities meet the criteria for being excepted from shutdown resides with the Secretaries of the Military Departments and Heads of the DoD Components, including the combatant commanders with respect to activities undertaken by their immediate headquarters and subordinate joint headquarters, who may delegate this authority as they deem appropriate. The attached guidance should be used to assist in making this determination. The guidance does not identify every excepted activity, but rather provides overarching direction and general principles for making these determinations. It should be applied prudently in the context of a Department at war, with decisions guaranteeing our continued robust support for those engaged in that war, and providing assurance that the lives and property of our Nation's citizens will be protected.

This memorandum contains guidance to begin detailed planning. No shutdown actions are to be taken until you receive further notice.

Within the Office of the Secretary of Defense, the Under Secretary of Defense (Comptroller) will take the lead in preparing for operations in the absence of appropriations, assisted by other offices as necessary.

To repeat, the Secretary and I hope that Congress will pass a funding bill and the DoD will avoid a shutdown. This guidance is intended to support prudent planning.

Patrick M. Shanahan

Attachment:
As stated

"The New Colossus"
By EMMA LAZARUS
November 2, 1883

Vol. 40   No. 20

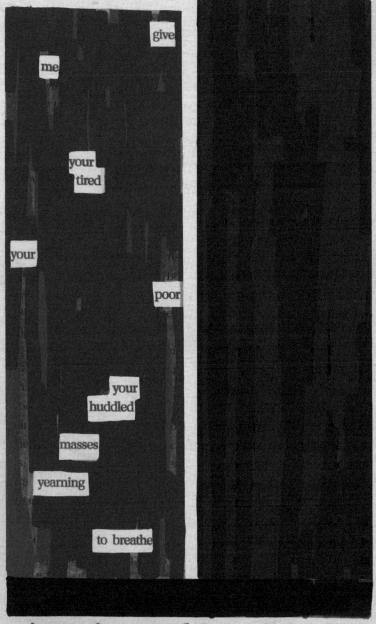

give
me
your
tired
your
poor
your
huddled
masses
yearning
to breathe

America and Immigration

**Letters from an American
Farmer: Letter III—
What Is an American.**
By J. HECTOR ST. JOHN DE
CRÈVECŒUR · Published 1782

LETTER III.

WHAT IS AN AMERICAN.

HE is an American, who, leaving behind him all his ancient prejudices and manners, receives new ones from the new mode of life he has embraced, the new government he obeys, and the new rank he holds. He becomes an American by being received in the broad lap of our great Alma Mater. Here individuals of all nations are melted into a new race of men, whose labours and posterity will one day cause great changes in the world. Americans are the western pilgrims, who are carrying along with them that great mass of arts, sciences, vigour, and industry which began long since in the east; they will finish the great circle. The Americans were once scattered all over Europe; here they are incorporated into one of the finest systems of population which has ever appeared, and which will hereafter become distinct by the power of the different climates they inhabit. The American ought therefore to love this country much better than that wherein either he or his forefathers were born. Here the rewards of his industry follow with equal steps the progress of his labour; his labour is founded

**Address on the occasion
of the fiftieth anniversary
of the Statue of Liberty**
Delivered by PRESIDENT FRANKLIN
D. ROOSEVELT · October 28, 1936

And the Almighty seems purposefully to have withheld that second chance until the time when men would most need and appreciate liberty, the time when men would be enlightened enough to establish it on foundations sound enough to maintain it.

For over three centuries a steady stream of men, women and children followed the beacon of liberty which this light symbolizes. They brought to us strength and moral fibre developed in a civilization centuries old but fired anew by the dream of a better life in America. They brought to one new country the cultures of a hundred old ones.

It has not been sufficiently emphasized in the teaching of our history that the overwhelming majority of those who came from the Nations of the Old World to our American shores were not the laggards, not the timorous, not the failures. They were men and women who had the supreme courage to strike out for themselves, to abandon language and relatives, to start at the bottom without influence, without money and without knowledge of life in a very young civilization. We can say for all America what the Californians say of the Forty-Niners: "The cowards never started and the weak died by the way."

Perhaps Providence did prepare this American continent to be a place of the second chance. Certainly, millions of men and women have made it that. They adopted this homeland because in this land they found a home in which the things they most desired could be theirs—freedom of opportunity, freedom of thought, freedom to worship God. Here they found life because here there was freedom to live.

It is the memory of all these eager seeking millions that makes this one of America's places of great romance. Looking down this great harbor I like to think of the countless numbers of inbound vessels that have made

Immigration Act of 1924
Enacted May 26, 1924

and seeking to enter temporarily the United States solely in the pursuit of his calling as a seaman, and (6) an alien entitled to enter the United States solely to carry on trade under and in pursuance of the provisions of a present existing treaty of commerce and navigation.

NON-QUOTA IMMIGRANTS.

Non-quota immigrants.

Sec. 4. When used in this Act the term "non-quota immigrant" means—

Term construed.

(a) An immigrant who is the unmarried child under 18 years of age, or the wife, of a citizen of the United States who resides therein at the time of the filing of a petition under section 9;

Minor child or wife of resident citizen applicant.
Post, p. 157.

(b) An immigrant previously lawfully admitted to the United States, who is returning from a temporary visit abroad;

Returning from temporary visit abroad.

(c) An immigrant who was born in the Dominion of Canada, Newfoundland, the Republic of Mexico, the Republic of Cuba, the Republic of Haiti, the Dominican Republic, the Canal Zone, or an independent country of Central or South America, and his wife, and his unmarried children under 18 years of age, if accompanying or following to join him;

Born in contiguous countries, Central or South America, etc.

(d) An immigrant who continuously for at least two years immediately preceding the time of his application for admission to the United States has been, and who seeks to enter the United States solely for the purpose of, carrying on the vocation of minister of any religious denomination, or professor of a college, academy, seminary, or university; and his wife, and his unmarried children under 18 years of age, if accompanying or following to join him; or

Ministers, etc., practicing profession two years preceding application.

(e) An immigrant who is a bona fide student at least 15 years of age and who seeks to enter the United States solely for the purpose of study at an accredited school, college, academy, seminary, or university, particularly designated by him and approved by the Secretary of Labor, which shall have agreed to report to the Secretary of Labor the termination of attendance of each immigrant student, and if any such institution of learning fails to make such reports promptly the approval shall be withdrawn.

Bona fide students. Conditions.

QUOTA IMMIGRANTS.

"Quota immigrants."

Sec. 5. When used in this Act the term "quota immigrant" means any immigrant who is not a non-quota immigrant. An alien who is not particularly specified in this Act as a non-quota immigrant or a non-immigrant shall not be admitted as a non-quota immigrant or a non-immigrant by reason of relationship to any individual who is so specified or by reason of being excepted from the operation of any other law regulating or forbidding immigration.

Means all nonquota immigrants.
Restriction of admissions as nonquota immigrants.

PREFERENCES WITHIN QUOTAS.

Preferences within quotas.

Sec. 6. (a) In the issuance of immigration visas to quota immigrants preference shall be given—

To be given in issuing visas.

(1) To a quota immigrant who is the unmarried child under 21 years of age, the father, the mother, the husband, or the wife, of a citizen of the United States who is 21 years of age or over; and

Specified relatives of a citizen.

(2) To a quota immigrant who is skilled in agriculture, and his wife, and his dependent children under the age of 16 years, if accompanying or following to join him. The preference provided in this paragraph shall not apply to immigrants of any nationality the annual quota for which is less than 300.

Skilled in agriculture.

Limitation.

First annual message
Delivered by PRESIDENT CALVIN
COOLIDGE · December 6, 1923

Mere intelligence, however, is not enough. Enlightenment must be accompanied by that moral power which is the product of the home and of rebellion. Real education and true welfare for the people rest inevitably on this foundation, which the Government can approve and commend, but which the people themselves must create.

IMMIGRATION

American institutions rest solely on good citizenship. They were created by people who had a background of self-government. New arrivals should be limited to our capacity to absorb them into the ranks of good citizenship. America must be kept American. For this purpose, it is necessary to continue a policy of restricted immigration. It would be well to make such immigration of a selective nature with some inspection at the source, and based either on a prior census or upon the record of naturalization. Either method would insure the admission of those with the largest capacity and best intention of becoming citizens. I am convinced that our present economic and social conditions warrant a limitation of those to be admitted. We should find additional safety in a law requiring the immediate registration of all aliens. Those who do not want to be partakers of the American spirit ought not to settle in America.

VETERANS

No more important duty falls on the Government of the United States than the adequate care of its veterans. Those suffering disabilities incurred in the service must have sufficient hospital relief and compensation. Their dependents must be supported. Rehabilitation and vocational training must be completed. All of this service must be clean, must be prompt and effective, and it must be administered in a spirit of the broadest and deepest human sympathy. If investigation reveals any present defects of administration or need of legislation, orders will be given for the immediate correction of administration, and recommendations for legislation should be given the highest preference.

Chinese Exclusion Act
Enacted May 6, 1882

Dr. Martin
American Civilization Since the Civil War
Spring Semester
MWF, 11:00-12:15

January 29, 1988

Chinese Exclusion Act

Weekly Essay Topic:
Summarize the events that led to the passage of the Chinese Exclusion Act and identify what effects the law had on anti-immigrant sentiment in the United States, particularly regarding those of Asian descent.

AN ACT TO EXECUTE CERTAIN TREATY STIPULATIONS RELATING TO CHINESE.

Whereas in the opinion of the Government of the United States the coming of Chinese laborers to this country endangers the good order of certain localities within the territory thereof: Therefore,

Be it enacted by the Senate and House of Representatives of the United States of America in Congress assembled, That from and after the expiration of ninety days next after the passage of this act, and until the expiration of ten years next after the passage of this act, the coming of Chinese laborers to the United States be, and the same is hereby, suspended; and during such suspension it shall not be lawful for any Chinese laborer to come, or having so come after the expiration of said ninety days to remain within the United States.

SEC. 2. That the master of any vessel who shall knowingly bring within the United States on such vessel, and land or permit to be landed, any Chinese laborer, from any foreign port or place, shall be deemed guilty of a misdemeanor, and on conviction thereof shall be punished by a fine of not more than five hundred dollars for each and every such Chinese laborer so brought, and maybe also imprisoned for a term not exceeding one year.

SEC. 3. That the two foregoing sections shall not apply to Chinese laborers who were in the United States on the seventeenth day of November, eighteen hundred and eighty, or who shall have come into the same before the expiration of ninety days next after the passage of this act, and who shall produce to such master before going on board such vessel, and shall produce to the collector of the port in the United States at which such vessel shall arrive, the evidence hereinafter in this act required of his being one of the laborers in this section mentioned; nor shall the two

Third annual message
Delivered by PRESIDENT WOODROW
WILSON · December 7, 1915

THIRD ANNUAL MESSAGE

by PRESIDENT WOODROW WILSON

I HAVE SPOKEN TO YOU TO-DAY, GENTLEMEN, upon a single theme, the thorough preparation of the nation to care for its own security and to make sure of entire freedom to play the impartial role in this hemisphere and in the world which we all believe to have been providentially assigned to it. I have had in my mind no thought of any immediate or particular danger arising out of our relations with other nations. We are at peace with all the nations of the world, and there is reason to hope that no question in controversy between this and other Governments will lead to any serious breach of amicable relations, grave as some differences of attitude and policy have been and may yet turn out to be. I am sorry to say that the gravest threats against our national peace and safety have been uttered within our own borders. There are citizens of the United States, I blush to admit, born under other flags but welcomed under our generous naturalization laws to the full freedom and opportunity of America, who have poured the poison of disloyalty into the very arteries of our national life; who have sought to bring the authority and good name of our Government into contempt, to destroy our industries wherever they thought it effective for their vindictive purposes to strike at them, and to debase our politics to the uses of foreign intrigue. Their number is not great as compared with the whole number of those sturdy hosts by which our nation has been enriched in recent generations out of virile foreign stock; but it is great enough to have brought deep disgrace upon us and to have made it necessary that we should promptly make use of processes of law by which we may be purged of their corrupt distempers. America never witnessed anything like this before. It never dreamed it possible that men sworn into its own citizenship, men drawn out of great free stocks such as supplied some of the best and strongest elements of that little, but how heroic, nation that in a high day of old staked its very life to free itself from every entanglement that had darkened the fortunes of the older nations and set up a new standard here, that men of such origins and such free choices of allegiance would ever turn in malign reaction against the Government and people who had welcomed and nurtured them and seek to make this proud country once more a hotbed of European passion. A little while ago such a thing would have seemed incredible. Because it was incredible we made no preparation for it. We would have been almost ashamed to prepare for it, as if we were suspicious of ourselves, our own comrades and neighbors! But the ugly and incredible thing has actually come about and we are without adequate federal laws to deal with it. I urge you to enact such laws at the earliest possible moment and feel that in doing so I am urging you to do nothing less than save the honor and self-respect of the nation. Such creatures of passion, disloyalty, and anarchy

**Remarks at the signing
of the Immigration and
Nationality Act at Liberty
Island, New York**
Delivered by PRESIDENT LYNDON B.
JOHNSON · October 3, 1965

PART IV

THE BEGINNINGS OF MODERN IMMIGRATION POLICY

In the final days of consideration, this bill had no more able champion than the present Attorney General, Nicholas Katzenbach, who, with New York's own "Manny" Celler, and Senator Ted Kennedy of Massachusetts, and Congressman Feighan of Ohio, and Senator Mansfield and Senator Dirksen constituting the leadership of the Senate, and Senator Javits, helped to guide this bill to passage, along with the help of the Members sitting in front of me today.

This bill says simply that from this day forth those wishing to immigrate to America shall be admitted on the basis of their skills and their close relationship to those already here.

This is a simple test, and it is a fair test. Those who can contribute most to this country—to its growth, to its strength, to its spirit—will be the first that are admitted to this land.

The fairness of this standard is so self-evident that we may well wonder that it has not always been applied. Yet the fact is that for over four decades the immigration policy of the United States has been twisted and has been distorted by the harsh injustice of the national origins quota system.

Under that system the ability of new immigrants to come to America depended upon the country of their birth. Only 3 countries were allowed to supply 70 percent of all the immigrants.

Families were kept apart because a husband or a wife or a child had been born in the wrong place.

Men of needed skill and talent were denied entrance because they came from southern or eastern Europe or from one of the developing continents.

This system violated the basic principle of American democracy—the principle that values and rewards each man on the basis of his merit as a man.

It has been un-American in the highest sense, because it has been untrue to the faith that brought thousands to these shores even

President Lyndon B. Johnson signs the Immigration Act as Vice President Hubert Humphrey, Lady Bird Johnson, Muriel Humphrey, Sen. Edward (Ted) Kennedy, Sen. Robert F. Kennedy, and others look on.

**Remarks by the president
in address to the nation
on immigration**
Delivered by PRESIDENT BARACK
OBAMA · November 20, 2014

nation that finds a way to welcome her in? Scripture tells us that we shall not oppress a stranger, for we know the heart of a stranger—we were strangers once, too.

My fellow Americans, we are and always will be a nation of immigrants. We were strangers once, too. And whether our forebears were strangers who crossed the Atlantic, or the Pacific, or the Rio Grande, we are here only because this country welcomed them in, and taught them that to be an American is about something more than what we look like, or what our last names are, or how we worship. What makes us Americans is our shared commitment to an ideal—that all of us are created equal, and all of us have the chance to make of our lives what we will.

That's the country our parents and

Memorandum
From: JOHN KELLY, SECRETARY
OF HOMELAND SECURITY
Subject: Enforcement of the
Immigration Laws to Serve the
National Interest · February 20, 2017

Homeland
Security

With the exception of the June 15, 2012, memorandum entitled "Exercising Prosecutorial Discretion with Respect to Individuals Who Came to the United States as Children," and the November 20, 2014 memorandum entitled "Exercising Prosecutorial Discretion with Respect to Individuals Who Came to the United States as Children and with Respect to Certain Individuals Who Are the Parents of U.S. Citizens or Permanent Residents,"[1] all existing conflicting directives, memoranda, or field guidance regarding the enforcement of our immigration laws and priorities for removal are hereby immediately rescinded—to the extent of the conflict—including, but not limited to, the November 20, 2014, memoranda entitled "Policies for the Apprehension, Detention and Removal of Undocumented Immigrants," and "Secure Communities."

A. The Department's Enforcement Priorities

Congress has defined the Department's role and responsibilities regarding the enforcement of the immigration laws of the United States. Effective immediately, and consistent with Article II, Section 3 of the United States Constitution and Section 3331 of Title 5, United States Code, Department personnel shall faithfully execute the immigration laws of the United States against all removable aliens.

Except as specifically noted above, the Department no longer will exempt classes or categories of removable aliens from potential enforcement. In faithfully executing the immigration laws, Department personnel should take enforcement actions in accordance with applicable law. In order to achieve this goal, as noted below, I have directed ICE to hire 10,000 officers and agents expeditiously, subject to available resources, and to take enforcement actions consistent with available resources. However, in order to maximize the benefit to public safety, to stem unlawful migration and to prevent fraud and misrepresentation, Department personnel should prioritize for removal those aliens described by Congress in Sections 212(a)(2), (a)(3), and (a)(6)(C), 235(b) and (c), and 237(a)(2) and (4) of the Immigration and Nationality Act (INA).

Additionally, regardless of the basis of removability, Department personnel should prioritize removable aliens who: (1) have been convicted of any criminal offense; (2) have been charged with any criminal offense that has not been resolved; (3) have committed acts which constitute a chargeable criminal offense; (4) have engaged in fraud or willful misrepresentation in connection with any official matter before a governmental agency; (5) have abused any program related to receipt of public benefits; (6) are subject to a final order of removal but have not complied with their legal obligation to depart the United States; or (7) in the judgment of an immigration officer, otherwise pose a risk to public safety or national security. The Director of ICE, the Commissioner of CBP, and the Director of USCIS may, as they determine is appropriate, issue further guidance to allocate appropriate resources to prioritize enforcement activities within these categories—for example, by prioritizing enforcement activities against removable aliens who are convicted felons or who are involved in gang activity or drug trafficking.

**Keynote speech to the Second
National Negro Congress**
Delivered by A. PHILIP RANDOLPH
1937

AMERICA & CIVIL RIGHTS

◆

favor of faits freedom
is
never
given.
it
is
won.

**The Meaning of July Fourth
for the Negro**
Delivered by FREDERICK DOUGLASS
July 5, 1852

The Meaning of July Fourth for the Negro

A speech given at Rochester, New York, July 5, 1852

Frederick Douglass
(1818(?)–1895)

. . . Fellow-citizens, pardon me, allow me to ask, why am I called upon to speak here to-day? What have I, or those I represent, to do with your national independence? Are the great principles of political freedom and of natural justice, embodied in that Declaration of Independence, extended to us? and am I, therefore, called upon to bring our humble offering to the national altar, and to confess the benefits and express devout gratitude for the blessings resulting from your independence to us?

Would to God, both for your sakes and ours, that an affirmative answer could be truthfully returned to these questions! Then would my task be light, and my burden easy and delightful. For who is there so cold, that a nation's sympathy could not warm him? Who so obdurate and dead to the claims of gratitude, that would not thankfully acknowledge such priceless benefits? Who so stolid and selfish, that would not give his voice to swell the hallelujahs of a nation's jubilee, when the chains of servitude had been torn from his limbs? I am not that man. In a case like that, the dumb might eloquently speak, and the "lame man leap as an hart."

But such is not the state of the case. I say it with a sad sense of the disparity between us. I am not included within the pale of glorious anniversary! Your high independence only reveals the immeasurable distance between us. The blessings in which you, this day, rejoice, are not enjoyed in common. The rich inheritance of justice, liberty, prosperity and independence, bequeathed by your fathers, is shared by you, not by me. The sunlight that brought light and healing to you, has brought stripes and death to me. This Fourth July is yours, not mine. You may rejoice, I must mourn. To drag a man in fetters into the grand illuminated temple of liberty, and call upon him to join you in joyous anthems, were inhuman mockery and sacrilegious irony. Do you mean, citizens, to mock me, by asking me to speak to-day?

Constitution of the United States
Written September 17, 1787
Ratified March 4, 1789

The Constitution

We the People
of the United States, in Order to form a more perfect Union, establish Justice, insure domestic Tranquility, provide for the common defence, promote the general Welfare, and secure the Blessings of Liberty to ourselves and our Posterity, do ordain and establish this CONSTITUTION for the United States of America.

Article. i.

SECTION. 1. All legislative Powers herein granted shall be vested in a Congress of the United States, which shall consist of a Senate and House of Representatives.

SECTION. 2. The House of Representatives shall be composed of Members chosen every second Year by the People of the several States, and the Electors in each State shall have the Qualifications requisite for Electors of the most numerous Branch of the State Legislature.

No Person shall be a Representative who shall not have attained to the Age of twenty five Years, and been seven Years a Citizen of the United States, and who shall not, when elected, be an Inhabitant of that State in which he shall be chosen.

Representatives and direct Taxes shall be apportioned among the several States which may be included within this Union, according to their respective Numbers, which shall be determined by adding to the whole Number of free Persons, including those bound to Service for a Term of Years, and excluding Indians not taxed, three fifths of all other Persons. The actual Enumeration shall be made within three Years after the first Meeting of the Congress of the United States, and within every subsequent Term of ten Years, in such Manner as they shall by Law direct. The Number of Representatives shall not exceed one for every thirty Thousand, but each State shall have at Least one Representative; and until such enumeration shall be made, the State of New Hampshire shall be entitled to choose three, Massachusetts eight, Rhode-Island and Providence Plantations one, Connecticut five, New-York six, New Jersey four, Pennsylvania eight, Delaware one, Maryland six, Virginia ten, North Carolina five, South Carolina five, and Georgia three.

When vacancies happen in the Representation from any State, the Executive Authority thereof shall issue Writs of Election to fill such Vacancies.

The House of Representatives shall choose their Speaker and other Officers; and shall have the sole Power of Impeachment.

Dred Scott v. Sandford,
US Supreme Court
Majority opinion delivered by
CHIEF JUSTICE ROGER TANEY
March 6, 1857

In the opinion of the court, the legislation and histories of the times, and the language used in the Declaration of Independence, show that neither the class of persons who had been imported as slaves nor their descendants, whether they had become free or not, were then acknowledged as a part of the people, nor intended to be included in the general words used in that memorable instrument.

It is difficult at this day to realize the state of public opinion in relation to that unfortunate race which prevailed in the civilized and enlightened portions of the world at the time of the Declaration of Independence and when the Constitution of the United States was framed and adopted. But the public history of every European nation displays it in a manner too plain to be mistaken.

They had for more than a century before been regarded as beings of an inferior order, and altogether unfit to associate with the white race either in social or political relations, and so far inferior that they had no rights which the white man was bound to respect, and that the negro might justly and lawfully be reduced to slavery for his benefit. He was bought and sold, and treated as an ordinary article of merchandise and traffic whenever a profit could be made by it. This opinion was at that time fixed and universal in the civilized portion of the white race. It was regarded as an axiom in morals as well as in politics which no one thought of disputing or supposed to be open to dispute, and men in every grade and position in society daily

First annual message to Congress

Delivered by PRESIDENT ANDREW JACKSON · December 8, 1829

Mr. Meyers   February 10, 1986
A.P. US History
5th Period

MIDTERM ESSAY TOPIC: Examine the following passage from President Jackson's
annual message to Congress. In this section, he expresses the belief that
Indian removal is the natural course of action to both make way for the
expansion of settlement in the West and to ensure the ongoing existence of
the Indian tribes. Write a 5-page essay considering whether this idea was
proven accurate or not. Use specific examples to make your case.

It will place a dense and civilized population in large tracts of country
now occupied by a few savage hunters. By opening the whole territory
between Tennessee on the north and Louisiana on the south to the settlement
of the whites it will incalculably strengthen the southwestern frontier and
render the adjacent States strong enough to repel future invasions without
remote aid. It will relieve the whole State of Mississippi and the western
part of Alabama of Indian occupancy, and enable those States to advance
rapidly in population, wealth, and power. It will separate the Indians from
immediate contact with settlements of whites; free them from the power of
the States; enable them to pursue happiness in their own way and under
their own rude institutions; will retard the progress of decay, which is
lessening their numbers, and perhaps cause them gradually, under the
protection of the Government and through the influence of good counsels, to
cast off their savage habits and become an interesting, civilized, and
Christian community.

What good man would prefer a country covered with forests and ranged by a
few thousand savages to our extensive Republic, studded with cities, towns,
and prosperous farms embellished with all the improvements which art can
devise or industry execute, occupied by more than 12,000,000 happy people,
and filled with all the blessings of liberty, civilization and religion?

The present policy of the Government is but a continuation of the same
progressive change by a milder process. The tribes which occupied the
countries now constituting the Eastern States were annihilated or have
melted away to make room for the whites. The waves of population and
civilization are rolling to the westward, and we now propose to acquire the
countries occupied by the red men of the South and West by a fair exchange,
and, at the expense of the United States, to send them to land where their
existence may be prolonged and perhaps made perpetual. Doubtless it will be

Dawes Act
Enacted February 8, 1887

Forty-Ninth Congress of the United States of America;

At the *Second* Session,

Begun and held at the City of Washington on Monday, the *sixth* day of December, one thousand eight hundred and eight-*six*.

AN ACT

to provide for the allotment of lands in severalty to Indians on the various reservations, and to extend the protection of the laws of the United States and the Territories over the Indians, and for other purposes.

Be it enacted *by the Senate and House of Representatives of the United States of America in Congress assembled, That* in all cases where any tribe or band of Indians has been, or shall hereafter be, located upon any reservation created for their use, either by treaty stipulation or by virtue of an act of Congress or executive order setting apart the same for their use, the President of the United States be, and he hereby is, authorized, whenever in his opinion any reservation or any part thereof of such Indians is advantageous for agricultural and grazing purposes, to cause said reservation, or any part thereof, to be surveyed, or resurveyed if necessary, and to allot the lands in said reservation in severalty to any Indian located thereon in quantities as follows:

> To each head of a family, one-quarter of a section;
> To each single person over eighteen years of age, one-eighth
> of a section;
> To each orphan child under eighteen years of age, one-eighth
> of a section; and
> To each other single person under eighteen years now living,
> or who may be born prior to the date of the order of the
> President directing an allotment of the lands embraced in
> any reservation, one-sixteenth of a section:

**An Indian's View
of Indian Affairs**
Delivered by CHIEF JOSEPH
April 1879

VOLUME VI—NO. 28   **GLENCOE, MINNESOTA • WEDNES**

CHIEF   JOSEPH   SPEAKS   OUT   AGAINST

The Indian Chief Joseph, leader of the Nez Percé tribe hailing from the Pacific Northwest region of the United States, delivered a stirring address detailing the harrowing and heartbreaking experiences endured when his people were forcibly removed from their ancestral lands. Here he accounts firsthand the actions white settlers took against the native peoples for the sake of land ownership.

* * *

When my father was a young man there came to our country a white man (Rev. Mr. Spaulding) who talked spirit law. He won the affections of our people because he spoke good things to them. At first he did not say anything about white men wanting to settle on our lands. Nothing was said about that until about twenty winters ago, when a number of white people came into our country and built houses and made farms. At first our people made no complaint. They thought there was room enough for all to live in peace, and they were learning many things from the white men that seemed to be good. But we soon found that the white men were growing rich very fast, and were greedy to possess

father's caution. He had sharper eyes than the rest of our people.

Next there came a white officer (Governor Stevens), who invited all the Nez Percés to a treaty council. After the council was opened he made known his heart. He said there were a great many white people in the country, and many more would come; that he wanted the land marked out so that the Indians and white men could be separated. If they were to live in peace it was necessary, he said, that the Indians should have a country set apart for them, and in that country they must stay. My father, who represented his band, refused to have anything to do with the council, because he wished to be a free man. He claimed that no man owned any part of the earth, and a man could not sell what he did not own.

Mr. Spaulding took hold of my father's arm and said, "Come and sign the treaty." My father pushed him away, and said: "Why do you ask me to sign away my country? It is your business to talk to us about spirit matters, and not to talk to us about parting with our land." Governor Stevens urged my father to sign his treaty, but he refused. "I will not sign your paper," he said; "you go where you please, so do I; you

Gettysburg Address
Delivered by PRESIDENT ABRAHAM
LINCOLN · November 19, 1863

LINCOLN

Celebrating the Birth of Abraham Lincoln

By ROBERT D. LYNN

Esteemed for his extraordi-
nary leadership during one of
America's most influential
periods, President Abraham
Lincoln successfully preserved
the Union and saw the country
through the Civil War, one of
the most politically, economi-
cally, and morally tumultuous
periods of American history.
On this day, February 12, we
celebrate his birthday in 1809.

The 6th president's iconic Gettysburg
Address is inscribed on the south wall of
the Lincoln Memorial in Washington, DC.

FOUR SCORE AND SEVEN YEARS AGO OUR FATHERS BROUGHT FORTH ON THIS CONTINENT A NEW NATION CONCEIVED IN LIBERTY AND DEDICATED TO THE PROPOSITION THAT ALL MEN ARE CREATED EQUAL · NOW WE ARE ENGAGED IN A GREAT CIVIL WAR TESTING WHETHER THAT NATION OR ANY NATION SO CONCEIVED AND SO DEDICATED CAN LONG ENDURE · WE ARE MET ON A GREAT BATTLEFIELD OF THAT WAR · WE HAVE COME TO DEDICATE A PORTION OF THAT FIELD AS A FINAL RESTING PLACE FOR THOSE WHO HERE GAVE THEIR LIVES THAT THAT NATION MIGHT LIVE · IT IS ALTOGETHER FITTING AND PROPER THAT WE SHOULD DO THIS · BUT IN A LARGER SENSE WE CAN NOT DEDICATE~WE CAN NOT CONSECRATE~WE CAN NOT HALLOW~THIS GROUND · THE BRAVE MEN LIVING AND DEAD WHO STRUGGLED HERE HAVE CONSECRATED IT FAR ABOVE OUR POOR POWER TO ADD OR DETRACT · THE WORLD WILL LITTLE NOTE NOR LONG REMEMBER WHAT WE SAY HERE BUT IT CAN NEVER FORGET WHAT THEY DID HERE · IT IS FOR US THE LIVING RATHER TO BE DEDICATED HERE TO THE UNFINISHED WORK WHICH THEY WHO FOUGHT HERE HAVE THUS FAR SO NOBLY ADVANCED · IT IS RATHER FOR US TO BE HERE DEDICATED TO THE GREAT TASK REMAINING BEFORE US~THAT FROM THESE HONORED DEAD WE TAKE INCREASED DEVOTION TO THAT CAUSE FOR WHICH THEY GAVE THE LAST FULL MEASURE OF DEVOTION ~ THAT WE HERE HIGHLY RESOLVE THAT THESE DEAD SHALL NOT HAVE DIED IN VAIN~THAT THIS NATION UNDER GOD SHALL HAVE A NEW BIRTH OF FREEDOM~AND THAT GOVERNMENT OF THE PEOPLE BY THE PEOPLE FOR THE PEOPLE SHALL NOT PERISH FROM THE EARTH ·

US Constitution,
Thirteenth Amendment
Passed by CONGRESS January 31, 1865
Ratified December 6, 1865

US Constitution,
Fourteenth Amendment
Passed by CONGRESS June 13, 1866
Ratified July 9, 1868

Mrs. Bradford   October 5, 1981
U.S. History
3rd Period

Judge the extent to which the ratification of the Reconstruction
Amendments (13th, 14th, & 15th) marked a turning point in the social
and political landscape of the United States. Give examples of what
changed and what stayed the same during the period immediately before
the amendments and the period immediately following their passage.

---

*remember to
synthesize and
vocabulary re*

AMENDMENT XIII

Section 1.
Neither slavery nor involuntary servitude, except as a punishment for
crime whereof the party shall have been duly convicted, shall exist
within the United States, or any place subject to their jurisdiction.

Section 2.
Congress shall have power to enforce this article by appropriate
legislation.

AMENDMENT XIV

Section 1.
All persons born or naturalized in the United States, and subject to
the jurisdiction thereof, are citizens of the United States and of the
State wherein they reside. No State shall make or enforce any law which
shall abridge the privileges or immunities of citizens of the United
States; nor shall any State deprive any person of life, liberty, or
property, without due process of law; nor deny to any person within
its jurisdiction the equal protection of the laws.

Section 2.
Representatives shall be apportioned among the several States
according to their respective numbers, counting the whole number of
persons in each State, excluding Indians not taxed. But when the right
to vote at any election for the choice of electors for President and
Vice-President of the United States, Representatives in Congress,
the Executive and Judicial officers of a State, or the members of the
Legislature thereof, is denied to any of the male inhabitants of such
State, being twenty-one years of age,* and citizens of the United

Lynch Law in All Its Phases
Delivered by IDA B. WELLS
February 13, 1893

Repeated attacks on the life, liberty and happiness of any citizen or class of citizens are attacks on distinctive American institutions; such attacks imperiling as they do the foundation of government, law and order, merit the thoughtful consideration of far-sighted Americans; not from a standpoint of sentiment, not even so much from a standpoint of justice to a weak race, as from a desire to preserve our institutions.

[2] THE RACE PROBLEM or negro question, as it has been called, has been omnipresent and all-pervading since long before the Afro-American was raised from the degradation of the slave to the dignity of the citizen. It has never been settled because the right methods have not been employed in the solution. It is the Banquo's ghost of politics, religion, and sociology which will not down at the bidding of those who are tormented with its ubiquitous appearance on every occasion. Times without number, since invested with citizenship, the race has been indicted for ignorance, immorality and general worthlessness declared guilty and executed by its self-constituted judges. The operations of law do not dispose of negroes fast enough, and lynching bees have become the favorite pastime of the South. As excuse for the same, a new cry, as false as it is foul, is raised in an effort to blast race character, a cry which has proclaimed to the world that virtue and innocence are violated by Afro-Americans who must be killed like wild beasts to protect womanhood and childhood.

[3] Born and reared in the South, I had never expected to live elsewhere. Until this past year I was one among those who believed the condition of the masses gave large excuse

Brown v. Board of Education,
US Supreme Court
Opinion delivered by CHIEF JUSTICE
EARL WARREN · May 17, 1954

Supreme Court of the United States

No. 1 —— , *October Term, 19* 54

Oliver Brown, Mrs. Richard Lawton, Mrs. Sadie Emmanuel et al.,
Appellants,

vs.

Board of Education of Topeka, Shawnee Country, Kansas, et al.

In *Sweatt v. Painter, supra,* in finding that a segregated law school
for Negroes could not provide them equal educational opportunities,
this Court relied in large part on "those qualities which are incapable
of objective measurement but which make for greatness in a law school."
In *McLaurin v. Oklahoma State Regents, supra,* the Court, in requiring
that a Negro admitted to a white graduate school be treated like all
other students, again resorted to intangible considerations: ". . .
his ability to study, to engage in discussions and exchange views
with other students, and, in general, to learn his profession." Such
considerations apply with added force to children in grade and high
schools. To separate them from others of similar age and qualifications
solely because of their race generates a feeling of inferiority as to
their status in the community that may affect their hearts and minds
in a way unlikely ever to be undone. The effect of this separation
on their educational opportunities was well stated by a finding in
the Kansas case by a court which nevertheless felt compelled to rule
against the Negro plaintiffs: Segregation of white and colored children
in public schools has a detrimental effect upon the colored children.
The impact is greater when it has the sanction of the law, for the
policy of separating the races is usually interpreted as denoting
the inferiority of the negro group. A sense of inferiority affects
the motivation of a child to learn. Segregation with the sanction of
law, therefore, has a tendency to [retard] the educational and mental
development of negro children and to deprive them of some of the
benefits they would receive in a racial[ly] integrated school system.
Whatever may have been the extent of psychological knowledge at the
time of *Plessy v. Ferguson,* this finding is amply supported by modern
authority. Any language in *Plessy v. Ferguson* contrary to this finding
is rejected.

We conclude that, in the field of public education, the doctrine
of "separate but equal" has no place. Separate educational facilities
are inherently unequal. Therefore, we hold that the plaintiffs and
others similarly situated for whom the actions have been brought are,

Special message to Congress
Delivered by PRESIDENT LYNDON B.
JOHNSON · March 15, 1965

We Shall Overcome

200,000 Voices Will Be Heard!

By ARTHUR E. HARTFORD

WASHINGTON, D.C.: President Lyndon Johnson urges Congress to pass voting rights legislation with a stirring speech praising the demonstrators campaigning for equal voting rights on March 7 in Selma, Alabama, and condemning the violence perpetrated on them by law enforcement. The president's passionate words call for the nation to take up the cause and ensure true freedom and equality for all its citizens.

We cannot, we must not, refuse to protect the right of every American to vote in every election that he may desire to participate in. And we ought not and we cannot and we must not wait another eight months before we get a bill. We have already waited a hundred years and more, and the time for waiting is gone.

So I ask you to join me in working long hours—nights and weekends, if necessary—to pass this bill. And I don't make that request lightly. For from the window where I sit with the problems of our country I recognize that from outside this chamber is the outraged conscience of a nation, the grave concern of many nations, and the harsh judgment of history on our acts. But even if we pass this bill, the battle will not be over. What happened in Selma is part of a far larger movement which reaches into every section and state of America. It is the effort of American Negroes to secure for themselves the full blessings of American life.

Their cause must be our cause, too. Because it is not just Negroes, but really it's all of us who must overcome the crippling legacy of bigotry and injustice.

And we shall overcome.

As a man whose roots go deeply into Southern soil I know how agonizing racial feelings are. I know how difficult it is to reshape the attitudes and the structure of our society.

But a century has passed, more than a hundred years, since the Negro was freed. And he is not fully free tonight.

It was more than a hundred years ago that Abraham Lincoln, a great president of another party, signed the Emancipation Proclamation, but emancipation is a proclamation and not a fact.

A century has passed, more than a hundred years, since equality was promised. And yet the Negro is not equal.

A century has passed since the day of promise. And the promise is unkept.

The time of justice has now come. I tell you that I believe sincerely that no force can hold it back. It is right in the eyes of man and God that it should come. And when it does, I think that day will brighten the lives of every American.

Remarks by the president on the fiftieth anniversary of the Selma to Montgomery marches
Delivered by PRESIDENT BARACK OBAMA · March 7, 2015

We know the march is not yet over. We know the race is not yet won. We know that reaching that blessed destination where we are judged, all of us, by the content of our character requires admitting as much, facing up to the truth. "We are capable of bearing a great burden," James Baldwin once wrote, "once we discover that the burden is reality and arrive where reality is."

There's nothing America can't handle if we actually look squarely at the problem. And this is work for all Americans, not just some. Not just whites. Not just blacks. If we want to honor the courage of those who marched that day, then all of us are called to possess their moral imagination. All of us will need to feel as they did the fierce urgency of now. All of us need to recognize as they did that change depends on our actions, on our attitudes, the things we teach our children. And if we make such an effort, no matter how hard it may sometimes seem, laws can be passed, and consciences can be stirred, and consensus can be built. (Applause.)

Korematsu v. United States,
US Supreme Court
Dissenting opinion delivered by
JUSTICE ROBERT JACKSON
December 18, 1944

SUPREME COURT OF THE UNITED STATES

Fred Toyosaburo Korematsu, Petitioner, *vs.* The United States of America.	On Writ of Certiorari to the United States Circuit Court of Appeals for the Ninth Circuit.

[December 18, 1944]

Mr. Justice JACKSON, dissenting.

I DISSENT, because I think the indisputable facts exhibit a clear violation of Constitutional rights.

This is not a case of keeping people off the streets at night, as was *Hirabayashi v. United States*, 320 U.S. 81, [p226] nor a case of temporary exclusion of a citizen from an area for his own safety or that of the community, nor a case of offering him an opportunity to go temporarily out of an area where his presence might cause danger to himself or to his fellows. On the contrary, it is the case of convicting a citizen as a punishment for not submitting to imprisonment in a concentration camp, based on his ancestry, and solely because of his ancestry, without evidence or inquiry concerning his loyalty and good disposition towards the United States. If this be a correct statement of the facts disclosed by this record, and facts of which we take judicial notice, I need hardly labor the conclusion that Constitutional rights have been violated.

The Government's argument, and the opinion of the court, in my judgment, erroneously divide that which is single and indivisible, and thus make the case appear as if the petitioner violated a Military Order, sanctioned by Act of Congress, which excluded him from his home by refusing voluntarily to leave, and so knowingly and intentionally defying the order and the Act of Congress.

The petitioner, a resident of San Leandro, Alameda County, California, is a native of the United States of Japanese ancestry who, according to the uncontradicted evidence, is a loyal citizen of the nation.

Memorandum
From: CLIFFORD L. STANLEY,
Under Secretary of Defense
Subject: Repeal of "Don't Ask, Don't
Tell" · September 20, 2011

UNDER SECRETARY OF DEFENSE
4000 DEFENSE PENTAGON
WASHINGTON, D.C. 20301-4000

SEP 20 2011

PERSONNEL AND
READINESS

MEMORANDUM FOR SEE DISTRIBUTION

SUBJECT: Repeal of "Don't Ask, Don't Tell"

The purpose of this memorandum is to inform you that the law commonly known as "Don't Ask, Don't Tell" (DADT), 10 U.S.C. Sec 654, is repealed and no longer in effect in the Department of Defense.

This repeal today follows the certification to Congress by the President, Secretary of Defense, and Chairman of the Joint Chiefs of Staff on July 22, 2011 that the Armed Forces were prepared to implement repeal in a manner consistent with the standards of military readiness, military effectiveness, unit cohesion, and recruiting and retention.

Effective today, statements about sexual orientation or lawful acts of homosexual conduct will not be considered as a bar to military service or admission to Service academies, ROTC or any other accession program. It remains the policy of the Department of Defense that sexual orientation is a personal and private matter. Applicants for enlistment or appointment may not be asked, or required to reveal, their sexual orientation. Sexual orientation may not be a factor in accession, promotion, separation, or other personnel decision-making.

All Service members are to treat one another with dignity and respect regardless of sexual orientation. Harassment or abuse based on sexual orientation is unacceptable and will be dealt with through command or inspector general channels. The Department of Defense is committed to promoting an environment free from personal, social, or institutional barriers that prevent Service members from rising to the highest level of responsibility possible regardless of sexual orientation. Gay and lesbian Service members, like all Service members, shall be evaluated only on individual merit, fitness, and capability.

Effective today, the Department of Defense and Services will implement their respective pre-approved policy and regulatory revisions effected by repeal. Additional policy guidance can be found in the attached memorandum dated January 28, 2011, "Repeal of Don't Ask, Don't Tell and Future Impact on Policy," and the September 20, 2011, "Repeal Implementation Quick Reference Guide."

Clifford L. Stanley

Attachments:
As stated

Obergefell v. Hodges,
US Supreme Court
Majority opinion delivered by
JUSTICE ANTHONY M. KENNEDY
June 26, 2015

Syllabus

OBERGEFELL ET AL. *v.* HODGES, DIRECTOR, OHIO
DEPARTMENT OF HEALTH, ET AL.

PEALS FOR

, 2015*

28   OBERGEFELL *v.* HODGES

Opinion of the Court

mote instability and uncertainty. For some couples, even
an ordinary drive into a neighboring State to visit family
or friends risks causing severe hardship in the event of a
spouse's hospitalization while across state lines. In light
of the fact that many States already allow same-sex mar-
riage—and hundreds of thousands of these marriages
already have occurred—the disruption caused by the
recognition bans is significant and ever-growing.

As counsel for the respondents acknowledged at argu-
ment, if States are required by the Constitution to issue
marriage licenses to same-sex couples, the justifications
for refusing to recognize those marriages performed else-
where are undermined. See Tr. of Oral Arg. on Question
2, p. 44. The Court, in this decision, holds same-sex cou-
ples may exercise the fundamental right to marry in all
States. It follows that the Court also must hold—and it
now does hold—that there is no lawful basis for a State to
refuse to recognize a lawful same-sex marriage performed
in another State on the ground of its same-sex character.

*   *   *

No union is more profound than marriage, for it embod-
ies the highest ideals of love, fidelity, devotion, sacrifice,
and family. In forming a marital union, two people be-
come something greater than once they were. As some of
the petitioners in these cases demonstrate, marriage
embodies a love that may endure even past death. It
would misunderstand these men and women to say they
disrespect the idea of marriage. Their plea is that they do
respect it, respect it so deeply that they seek to find its
fulfillment for themselves. Their hope is not to be con-
demned to live in loneliness, excluded from one of civiliza-
tion's oldest institutions. They ask for equal dignity in the
eyes of the law. The Constitution grants them that right.

The judgment of the Court of Appeals for the Sixth
Circuit is reversed.

It is so ordered.

Ruth Bader Ginsburg, in an interview with *USA Today*
May 5, 2009

American Women

women

belong

in

all

places

Where

Decisions

are

being

made

**Letter from Abigail Adams
to John Adams**
March 31, 1776

I feel a gaieti de Coar to which before I was a stranger. I think the Sun looks brighter, the Birds sing more melodiously, and Nature puts on a more chearfull countanance. We feel a temporary peace, and the poor fugitives are returning to their deserted habitations.

Tho we felicitate ourselves, we sympathize with those who are trembling least the Lot of Boston should be theirs. But they cannot be in similar circumstances unless pusilanimity and cowardise should take possession of them. They have time and warning given them to see the Evil and shun it.—I long to hear that you have declared an independancy—and by the way in the new Code of Laws which I suppose it will be necessary for you to make I desire you would Remember the Ladies, and be more generous and favourable to them than your ancestors. Do not put such unlimited power into the hands of the Husbands. Remember all Men would be tyrants if they could. If perticuliar care and attention is not paid to the Laidies we are determined to foment a Rebelion, and will not hold ourselves bound by any Laws in which we have no voice, or Representation.

That your Sex are Naturally Tyrannical is a Truth so thoroughly established as to admit of no dispute, but such of you as wish to be happy willingly give up the harsh title of Master for the more tender and endearing one of Friend. Why then, not put it out of the power of the vicious and the Lawless to use us with cruelty and indignity with impunity. Men of Sense in all Ages abhor those customs which treat us only as the vassals of your Sex. Regard us then as Beings placed by providence under your protection and in immitation of the Supreem Being make use of that power only for our happiness.

**Remarks to the Committee
of the Judiciary of the United
States Congress**
Delivered by ELIZABETH CADY
STANTON · January 18, 1892

VOICES FROM HISTORY

Elizabeth Cady Stanton
"Solitude of Self"

Elizabeth Cady Stanton was a primary leader of the women's suffrage movement in the United States as well as one of the most renowned feminists of her generation. In her classic Solitude of Self speech to Congress in 1892, Stanton passionately articulated the arguments for women's equality she had spent a lifetime advocating for.

They manage the laundries; they are now considered our best milliners and dressmakers. Because some men fill these departments of usefulness, shall we regulate the curriculum in Harvard and Yale to their present necessities? If not, why this talk in our best colleges of a curriculum for girls who are crowding into the trades and professions, teachers in all our public schools, rapidly filling many lucrative and honorable positions in life?" . . .

Women are already the equals of men in the whole realm of thought, in art, science, literature and government. . . . The poetry and novels of the century are theirs, and they have touched the keynote of reform, in religion, politics and social life. They fill the editor's and professor's chair, plead at the bar of justice, walk the wards of the hospital, speak from the pulpit and the platform. Such is the type of womanhood that an enlightened public sentiment welcomes today, and such the triumph of the facts of life over the false theories of the past.

Is it, then, consistent to hold the developed woman of this day within the same narrow political limits as the dame with the spinning wheel and knitting needle occupied in the past? No, no! Machinery has taken the labors of woman as well as man on its tireless shoulders; the loom and the spinning wheel are but dreams of the past; the pen, the brush, the easel, the chisel, have taken their places, while the hopes and ambitions of women are essentially changed.

We see reason sufficient in the outer conditions of human beings for individual liberty and development, but when we consider the self-dependence of every human soul,

Nineteenth Amendment
Passed by CONGRESS June 4, 1919
Ratified August 18, 1920

5

AMENDMENT XIX

The right of citizens of the United States to vote
shall not be denied or abridged by the
United States or by any State on account of sex.

Congress shall have power to enforce this
article by appropriate legislation.

Remarks to the Senate
Delivered by REBECCA LATIMER
FELTON · November 22, 1922

Rebecca Latimer Felton

TO THE SENATE [1]

November 22, 1922

(In the Senate)

Mr. President, in my very remarkable campaign in Georgia, which, contrary to precedent, all came along after I was selected, one of the very amusing things that came to me by mail was a cartoon from San Antonio, Texas. The cartoon represented the United States Senate in session. The seats seemed to be fully occupied, and there appeared in the picture the figure of a woman who had evidently entered without sending in her card. The gentlemen in the Senate took the situation variously. Some seemed to be a little bit hysterical, but most of them occupied their time looking at the ceiling. Over the cartoon was written the wonderful words, "Will they ask the lady to take a chair?" [Laughter.] I want to return my thanks today for the beautiful, hospitable welcome that you have accorded to the lady when you gave her a chair.

I also want to return thanks to the noble men of Georgia. Georgia was very slow in her promises with reference to woman's suffrage. She has been rapid to perform, for Georgia is the first state in the federal Union composed of 48 states where one chivalric governor went to the front and said, "Send that old lady there and let her look at the Senate for even a day."

The senator-elect from Georgia, Mr. GEORGE,[2] said, "She shall have her day there," and I want to thank him in this presence. He is a worthy successor. I want to plead for your gracious attention to him. He has been most chivalric. The sitting senator from Georgia [Mr. HARRIS] [3] has been most obliging. Indeed, I feel that I am the happiest woman in the United States. I am at home in the Senate for a day. I appreciate this wonderful hospitality and the beautiful attention thus accorded to me.

I want to say further that I commend to your attention the ten million women voters who are watching this incident. It is a romantic incident, senators, but it is also a historical event. If Lady Astor,[4] from the state of Virginia, can go to London and be accepted as a member of the British House of Commons, you can take this remnant of the old South that has never flickered in her patriotism to her country and be very well assured that she is not going to discredit her commission.

Let me say, Mr. President, that when the women of the country come in and sit with you, though there may be but very few in the next few years, I pledge you that you will get ability, you will get integrity of purpose, you will get exalted patriotism, and you will get unstinted usefulness.

Mr. President and senators, I thank you very much for this hearing. [Applause on the floor and in the galleries.]

---

[1] U.S., Congress, Senate, *Congressional Record*, 67th Cong., 3d sess., p. 23.

[2] Walter F. George (1878–1957) served in the Senate, 1922–1957.

[3] William J. Harris (1868–1932) served in the Senate, 1919–1932.

[4] Nancy Langhorne Astor (1879–1964) succeeded her husband, Viscount Waldorf Astor, in the House of Commons when he moved to the House of Lords. She was the first woman member of Parliament.

Equal Rights Amendment
Passed by CONGRESS March 22, 1972
Never ratified

PROPOSED AMENDMENT

TO THE

CONSTITUTION OF THE UNITED STATES

SECOND SESSION, NINETY-SECOND CONGRESS

JOINT RESOLUTION

Proposing an amendment to the Constitution of the United States relative to [H. J. R
equal rights for men and women.

Resolved by the Senate and House of Representatives of the United States of America in Congress assembled (two-thirds of each House concurring therein), That the following article is proposed as an amendment to the Constitution of the United States, which shall be valid to all intents and purposes as part of the Constitution when ratified by the legislatures of three-fourths of the several States within seven years from the date of its submission by the Congress:

"ARTICLE —

"SECTION 1. Equality of rights under the law shall not be denied or abridged by the United States or by any State on account of sex.

"SEC. 2. The Congress shall have the power to enforce, by appropriate legislation, the provisions of this article.

"SEC. 3. This amendment shall take effect two years after the date of ratification."

CARL ALBERT

Speaker of the House of Representatives.

ALLEN J. ELLENDER

President of the Senate pro Tempore.

I certify that this Joint Resolution originated in the House of Representatives.

W. PAT JENNINGS

Clerk.

BY W. RAYMOND COLLEY

**Title IX of the Education
Amendments of 1972**
Chapter 38, Sec. 1681. Sex
Enacted June 23, 1972

26 June 1972

Memorandum

TO : All Employees of the
University Athletic Department

FROM : Office of the Provost

SUBJECT : RE: Education Amendments

Please see the newly enacted portion of the Education Amendments regarding sex discrimination in education activities. Note that this policy will be enforced when regular classes resume in September.

Sec. 1681. Sex

(a) Prohibition against discrimination; exceptions

No person in the United States shall, on the basis of sex, be excluded from participation in, be denied the benefits of, or be subjected to discrimination under any education program or activity receiving Federal financial assistance, except that:

(1)   Classes of educational institutions subject to prohibition in regard to admissions to educational institutions, this section shall apply only to institutions of vocational education, professional education, and graduate higher education, and to public institutions of undergraduate higher education;

(2)   Educational institutions commencing planned change in admissions in regard to admissions to educational institutions, this section shall not apply

(A) for one year from June 23, 1972, nor for six years after June 23, 1972, in the case of an educational institution which has begun the process of changing from being an institution which admits only students of one sex to being an institution which admits students of both sexes, but only if it is carrying out a plan for such a change which is approved by the Secretary of Education or

(B) for seven years from the date an educational institution begins the process of changing from being an institution which admits only students of only one sex to being an institution which admits students of both sexes, but only if it is carrying out a plan for such a change which is approved by the Secretary of Education, whichever is the later;

Roe v. Wade, **US Supreme Court**
Majority opinion delivered by
JUSTICE HARRY A. BLACKMUN
January 22, 1973

These decisions make it clear that only personal rights that can be
deemed "fundamental" or "implicit in the concept of ordered liberty,"
Palko v. Connecticut, 302 U. S. 319, 325 (1937), are included in this
guarantee of personal privacy. They also make it clear that the
right has some extension to activities relating to marriage, *Loving
v. Virginia*, 388 U. S. 1, 12 (1967); procreation, *Skinner v. Oklahoma*,
316 U. S. 535, 541-542 (1942); contraception, *Eisenstadt v. Baird*, 405
U.S. at 453-454; id. at 460, 463-465 (WHITE, J., concurring in result);
family relationships, Prince v. Massachusetts, 321 U. S. 158, 166 (1944);
and childrearing and education, Pierce v. Society of Sisters, 268 U. S.
510, 535 (1925), Meyer v. Nebraska, supra.

ROE ET ALL V. WADE
SUPREME COURT OF THE UNITED STATES

This right of privacy, whether it be founded in the Fourteenth
Amendment's concept of personal liberty and restrictions
upon state action, as we feel it is, or, as the District Court
determined, in the Ninth Amendment's reservation of rights to
the people, is broad enough to encompass a woman's decision
whether or not to terminate her pregnancy. The detriment
that the State would impose upon the pregnant woman by
denying this choice altogether is apparent. Specific and direct
harm medically diagnosable even in early pregnancy may
be involved. Maternity, or additional offspring, may force
upon the woman a distressful life and future. Psychological
harm may be imminent. Mental and physical health may
be taxed by child care. There is also the distress, for all
concerned, associated with the unwanted child, and there is
the problem of bringing a child into a family already unable,
psychologically and otherwise, to care for it. In other cases,
as in this one, the additional difficulties and continuing
stigma of unwed motherhood may be involved. All these are
factors the woman and her responsible physician necessarily
will consider in consultation.

On the basis of elements such as these, appellant and some
amici argue that the woman's right is absolute and that she

House Resolution 4155
Congressional Sexual Harassment
Training Act
Introduced October 26, 2017

115TH CONGRESS
1ST SESSION

H.R. 4155

A BILL

To amend the Congressional Accountability Act of 1995 to require employing offices under such Act to enroll the employees of such offices every two years in the program carried out by the Office of Compliance to train employees in the protections against sexual harassment provided under the Act, and for other purposes.

Be it enacted by the Senate and House of Representatives of the United States of America in Congress assembled,

SECTION 1. SHORT TITLE.

This Act may be cited as the "Congressional Sexual Harassment Training Act."

SECTION 2. REQUIRING EMPLOYING OFFICES UNDER CONGRESSIONAL ACCOUNTABILITY ACT OF 1995 TO ENROLL EMPLOYEES IN OFFICE OF COMPLIANCE PROGRAMS ON SEXUAL HARASSMENT.

(a) Mandatory Enrollment In Programs.—Part E of title II of the Congressional Accountability Act of 1995 (2 U.S.C. 1361 et seq.) is amended by adding at the end the following new section:

"SEC. 226. MANDATORY ENROLLMENT OF EMPLOYEES IN OFFICE OF COMPLIANCE PROGRAMS ON SEXUAL HARASSMENT.

"(a) Biennial Training For Employees Of Employing Offices.—Each employing office shall ensure that each covered employee of the employing office enrolls every two years in the program of education carried out by the Office of Compliance under section 301(h) to inform covered employees of the rights provided under this Act against sexual harassment.

"(b) Additional Initial Training.—In addition to the biennial enrollment required under subsection (a), each employing office shall ensure that each covered employee of the employing office enrolls in the program described in subsection (a) not later than—

"(1) in the case of a covered employee who is a covered employee of the employing office as of the date of the

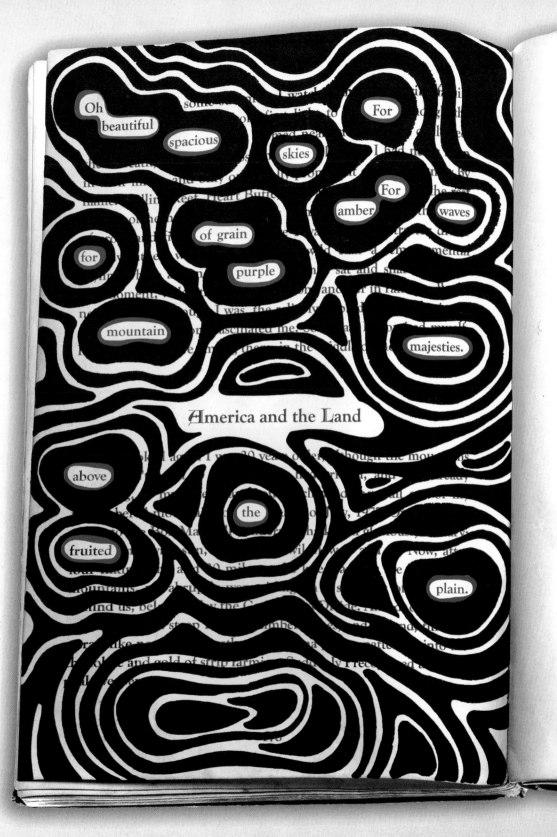

Oh beautiful spacious skies For For amber waves of grain for purple mountain majesties.

America and the Land

above the fruited plain.

Homestead Act
Enacted May 20, 1862

CHAP. LXXV. — *An Act to secure Homesteads to actual Settlers on the Public Domain.*

Be it enacted by the Senate and House of Representatives of the United States of America in Congress assembled, That any person who is the head of a family, or who has arrived at the age of twenty-one years, and is a citizen of the United States, or who shall have filed his declaration of intention to become such, as required by the naturalization laws of the United States, and who has never borne arms against the United States Government or given aid and comfort to its enemies, shall, from and after the first January, eighteen hundred and sixty-three, be entitled to enter one quarter section or a less quantity of unappropriated public lands, upon which said person may have filed a preemption claim, or which may, at the time the application is made, be subject to preemption at one dollar and twenty-five cents, or less, per acre; or eighty acres or less of such unappropriated lands, at two dollars and fifty cents per acre, to be located in a body, in conformity to the legal subdivisions of the public lands, and after the same shall have been surveyed: *Provided,* That any person owning and residing on land may, under the provisions of this act, enter other land lying contiguous to his or her said land, which shall not, with the land so already owned and occupied, exceed in the aggregate one hundred and sixty acres.

SEC. 2 *And be it further enacted,* That the person applying for the benefit of this act shall, upon application to the register of the land office in which he or she is about to make such entry, make affidavit before the said register or receiver that he or she is the head of a family, or is twenty-one years or more of age, or shall have performed service in the army or navy of the United States, and that he has never borne arms against the Government of the United States or given aid and comfort to its enemies, and that such application is made for his or her exclusive use and benefit, and that said entry is made for the purpose of actual settlement and cultivation, and not either directly or indirectly for the use or benefit of any other person or persons whomsoever:

The Frontier in American History
By FREDERICK JACKSON TURNER
1920

From the conditions of frontier life came intellectual traits of profound importance. The works of travelers along each frontier from colonial days onward describe certain common traits, and these traits have, while softening down, still persisted as survivals in the place of their origin, even when a higher social organization succeeded. The result is that to the frontier the American intellect owes its striking characteristics. That coarseness and strength combined with acuteness and inquisitiveness; that practical, inventive turn of mind, quick to find expedients; that masterful grasp of material things, lacking in the artistic but powerful to effect great ends; that restless, nervous energy; that dominant individualism, working for good and for evil, and withal that buoyancy and exuberance which comes with freedom—these are traits of the frontier, or traits called out elsewhere because of the existence of the frontier. Since the days when the fleet of Columbus sailed into the waters of the New World, America has been another name for opportunity, and the people of the United States have taken their tone from the incessant expansion which has not only been open but has even been forced upon them. He would be a rash prophet who should assert that the expansive character of American life has now entirely ceased. Movement has been its dominant fact, and, unless this training has no effect upon a people, the American energy will continually demand a wider field for its exercise. But never again will such gifts of free land offer themselves. For a moment, at the frontier, the bonds of custom are broken and unrestraint is triumphant. There is not tabula rasa. The stubborn American environment is there with its imperious summons to accept its conditions; the inherited ways of doing things are also there; and yet, in spite of environment, and in spite of custom, each frontier did indeed furnish a new field of opportunity, a gate of escape from the bondage of the past; and freshness, and confidence, and scorn of older society, impatience of its restraints and its ideas, and indifference to its lessons, have accompanied the frontier. What the Mediterranean Sea was to the Greeks, breaking the bond of custom, offering new experiences, calling out new institutions and activities, that, and more, the ever retreating frontier has been to the United States directly, and to the nations of Europe more remotely. And now, four centuries from the discovery of America, at the end of a hundred years of life under the Constitution, the frontier has

Antiquities Act of 1906
Enacted June 8, 1906

AMERICAN ANTIQUITIES ACT OF 1906

16 USC 431-433

Be it enacted by the Senate and House of Representatives of the United States of America in Congress assembled, That any person who shall appropriate, excavate, injure, or destroy any historic or prehistoric ruin or monument, or any object of antiquity, situated on lands owned or controlled by the Government of the United States, without the permission of the Secretary of the Department of the Government having jurisdiction over the lands on which said antiquities are situated, shall, upon conviction, be fined in a sum of not more than five hundred dollars or be imprisoned for a period of not more than ninety days, or shall suffer both fine and imprisonment, in the discretion of the court.

Sec. 2. That the President of the United States is hereby authorized, in his discretion, to declare by public proclamation historic landmarks, historic and prehistoric structures, and other objects of historic or scientific interest that are situated upon the lands owned or controlled by the Government of the United States to be national monuments, and may reserve as a part thereof parcels of land, the limits of which in all cases shall be confined to the smallest area compatible with proper care and management of the objects to be protected: Provided, That when such objects are situated upon a tract covered by a bona fied unperfected claim or held in private ownership, the tract, or so much thereof as may be necessary for the proper care and management of the object, may be relinquished to the Government, and the Secretary of the Interior is hereby authorized to accept the relinquishment of such tracts in behalf of the Government of the United States.

Sec. 3. That permits for the examination of ruins, the excavation of archaeological sites, and the gathering of objects of antiquity upon the lands under their respective jurisdictions may be granted by the Secretaries of the Interior, Agriculture, and War to institutions which the may deem properly qualified to conduct such examination, excavation, or gathering, subject to such rules and regulation as they may prescribe: Provided, That the examinations, excavations, and gatherings are undertaken for the benefit of reputable museums, universities, colleges, or other recognized scientific or educational institutions, with a view to increasing the knowledge of such objects, and that the gatherings shall be made for permanent preservation in public museums.

Remarks on Antiquities Act designations
Delivered by PRESIDENT DONALD J.
TRUMP · December 4, 2017

Thank you.

But before I began — because I understood how big it is — I'm a real estate developer. When they start talking about millions of acres, I say, say it again? That's a lot. So, before I began, I met with Senator Orrin Hatch, who loves Utah and loves the people of Utah. I called Senator Mike Lee, who loves Utah and loves the people of Utah. I called your governor. I called my original — where is he? There he is. I called all of the friends that I have in Utah. I said, what do you think? I said, will this be good for our country, and will it be good for your state? They said this would be incredible for our country, will be incredible for Utah. Finally, you would be giving people back their access to the land they know, to the land they understand, and most importantly, to the land that they love.

I also said, will it be at all controversial? They all told me no. (Laughter.) How did that happen? I don't think it is controversial, actually. I think it's so sensible.

Therefore, today, on the recommendation of Secretary Zinke, and with the wise counsel of Senator Hatch, Senator Lee, and the many others, I will sign two presidential proclamations. These actions will modify the national monuments designations of both Bears Ears and Grand Staircase-Escalante. (Applause.)

As many of you know, past administrations have severely abused the purpose, spirit, and intent of a century-old law known as the Antiquities Act. This law requires that only the smallest necessary area be set aside for special protection as national monuments. Unfortunately, previous administrations have ignored the standard and used the law to lock up hundreds of millions of acres of land and water under strict government control.

These abuses of the Antiquities Act give enormous power to faraway bureaucrats at the expense of the people who actually live here, work here, and make this place their home. This is where they raise their children. This is the place they love.

For example, the previous administration designated more than a half a billion acres of land and water, including Bears Ears. It did so over the loud objections of the people of this state and their elected representatives. Governor — right?

The results have been very sad and very predictable. Here, and in other affected states, we have seen harmful and unnecessary restrictions on hunting, ranching, and responsible economic development. We have seen grazing restrictions prevent ranching families from passing their businesses and beloved heritage on to the children — the children that they love.

We've seen many rural families stopped from enjoying their outdoor activities. And the fact they've done it all their lives made no difference to the bureaucrats in Washington.

We have seen needed improvements, like infrastructure upgrades and road maintenance, impeded and foreclosed. We have seen how this tragic federal overreach prevents many Native Americans from having their rightful voice over the sacred land where they practice their most important ancestral and religious traditions. (Applause.)

These abuses of the Antiquities Act have not just threatened your local economies; they've threatened your very way of life. They've threatened your hearts.

Our precious national treasures must be protected. And they, from now on, will be protected. (Applause.)

**Keynote address to the 1908
Conference of Governors**
Delivered by PRESIDENT THEODORE
ROOSEVELT · May 13, 1908

KEYNOTE ADDRESS

TO THE

1908 CONFERENCE OF GOVERNORS

Delivered by President Theodore Roosevelt

1. *Governors of the several States; and Gentlemen:*

2. I welcome you to this Conference at the White House. You have come hither at my request, so that we may join together to consider the question of the conservation and use of the great fundamental sources of wealth of this Nation.

3. So vital is this question, that for the first time in our history the chief executive officers of the States separately, and of the States together forming the Nation, have met to consider it. It is the chief material question that confronts us, second only—and second always—to the great fundamental questions of morality. [Applause]

4. With the governors come men from each State chosen for their special acquaintance with the terms of the problem that is before us. Among them are experts in natural resources and representatives of national organizations concerned in the development and use of these resources; the Senators and Representatives in Congress; the Supreme Court, the Cabinet, and the Inland Waterways Commission have likewise been invited to the Conference, which is therefore national in a peculiar sense.

5. This Conference on the conservation of natural resources is in effect a meeting of the representatives of all the people of the United States called to consider the weightiest problem now before the Nation; and the occasion for the meeting lies in the fact that the natural resources of our country are in danger of exhaustion if we permit the old wasteful methods of exploiting them longer to continue.

6. With the rise of peoples from savagery to civilization, and with the consequent growth in the extent and variety of the needs of the average man, there comes a steadily increasing growth of the amount demanded by this average man from the actual resources of the country. And yet, rather curiously, at the same time that there comes that increase in what the average man demands from the resources, he is apt to grow to lose the sense of his dependence upon nature. He lives in big cities. He deals in industries that do not bring him in close touch with nature. He does not realize the demands he is making upon nature. For instance, he finds, as he has found before in many

**Special Message to the Congress
about Reorganization Plans to
Establish the Environmental
Protection Agency and
the National Oceanic and
Atmospheric Administration**
Delivered by PRESIDENT RICHARD
NIXON · July 9, 1970

REORGANIZATION PLAN NO. 3
of 1970
ENVIRONMENTAL PROTECTION AGENCY

Submitted: July 9, 1970

TO THE CONGRESS of the UNITED STATES:

As concern with the condition of our physical environment has intensified, it has become increasingly clear that we need to know more about the total environment—land, water, and air. It also has become increasingly clear that only by reorganizing our Federal efforts can we develop that knowledge, and effectively ensure the protection, development and enhancement of the total environment itself.

The Government's environmentally-related activities have grown up piecemeal over the years. The time has come to organize them rationally and systematically. As a major step in this direction, I am transmitting today two reorganization plans: one to establish an Environmental Protection Agency, and one to establish, with the Department of Commerce, a National Oceanic and Atmospheric Administration.

ENVIRONMENTAL PROTECTION AGENCY
(EPA)

Our national government today is not structured to make a coordinated attack on the pollutants which debase the air we breathe, the water we drink, and the land that grows our food. Indeed, the present governmental structure for dealing with environmental pollution often defies effective and concerted action.

... for pollution control

**Remarks at the Kyoto Climate
Change Conference**
Delivered by VICE PRESIDENT
AL GORE · December 8, 1997

We have reached a fundamentally new stage in the development of human civilization, in which it is necessary to take responsibility for a recent but profound alteration in the relationship between our species and our planet. Because of our new technological power and our growing numbers, we now must pay careful attention to the consequences of what we are doing to the Earth—especially to the atmosphere.

There are other parts of the Earth's ecological system that are also threatened by the increasingly harsh impact of thoughtless behavior:

The poisoning of too many places where people—especially poor people—live, and the deaths of too many children—especially poor children—from polluted water and dirty air; the dangerous and unsustainable depletion of ocean fisheries; and the rapid destruction of critical habitats—rain forests, temperate forests, boreal forests, wetlands, coral reefs, and other precious wellsprings of genetic variety upon which the future of humankind depends.

But the most vulnerable part of the Earth's environment is the very thin layer of air clinging near to the surface of the planet, that we are

Climate Science Special Report:
Fourth National Climate
Assessment, **Volume I**
By the US GLOBAL CHANGE
RESEARCH PROGRAM,
Washington, DC · June 2017

Highlights of the U.S. Global Change Research Program Climate Science Special Report

The climate of the United States is strongly connected to the changing global climate. The statements below highlight past, current, and projected climate changes for the United States and the globe.

Global annually averaged surface air temperature has increased by about 1.8°F (1.0°C) over the last 115 years (1901–2016). **This period is now the warmest in the history of modern civilization.** The last few years have also seen record-breaking, climate-related weather extremes, and the last three years have been the warmest years on record for the globe. These trends are expected to continue over climate timescales.·

This assessment concludes, based on extensive evidence, that it is extremely likely that **human activities, especially emissions of greenhouse gases, are the dominant cause of the observed warming since the mid-20th century.** For the warming over the last century, there is no convincing alternative explanation supported by the extent of the observational evidence.

In addition to warming, many other aspects of global climate are changing, primarily in response to human activities. **Thousands of studies conducted by researchers around the world have documented changes in surface, atmospheric, and oceanic temperatures; melting glaciers; diminishing snow cover; shrinking sea ice; rising sea levels; ocean acidification; and increasing atmospheric water vapor.**

For example, **global average sea level has risen by about 7–8 inches** since 1900, with almost half (about 3 inches) of that rise occurring since 1993. Human-caused climate change has made a substantial contribution to this rise since 1900, contributing to a rate of rise that is greater than during any preceding century in at least 2,800 years. Global sea level rise has already affected the United States; **the incidence of daily tidal flooding is accelerating in more than 25 Atlantic and Gulf Coast cities.**

Global average sea levels are expected to continue to rise—by at least several inches in the next 15 years and by 1–4 feet by 2100. A rise of as much as 8 feet by 2100 cannot be ruled out. Sea level rise will be higher than the global average on the East and Gulf Coasts of the United States.

Changes in the characteristics of extreme events are particularly important for human safety, infrastructure, agriculture, water quality and quantity, and natural ecosystems. **Heavy rainfall is increasing in intensity and frequency across the United States and globally and is expected to continue to increase.** The largest observed changes in the United States have occurred in the Northeast.

Foreword by Jerrod Schwarz

Design by Katie Benezra, Tree Abraham, Lindsay Bazos, and Melissa Faustine

Section opening art created by Talia Behrend-Wilcox, Madeline Jaffe, Shawn Dahl, Karrie Witkin, and Rebecca Westall

Background Photography: Pages 4–5 Pichet siritantiwat/Shutterstock.com. Pages 6–7: Jiri Hera/Shutterstock.com. Pages 10–11: I. Pilon/Shutterstock.com, Everett Historical/Shutterstock.com. Pages 16–17: santol/Shutterstock.com, Baimieng/ Shutterstock.com. Pages 22–23: Feng Yu/Shutterstock.com, redstone/Shutterstock. com. Pages 26–27: Daboost/Shutterstock.com. Pages 44–45: Nagornyi/Shutterstock. com. Pages 72–73: Feng Yu/Shutterstock.com, redstone/Shutterstock.com. Pages 86–87: Daboost/Shutterstock.com. Pages 92–93: Valentin Agapov/Shutterstock. com. Pages 94–95: Everett Historical/Shutterstock.com. Pages 104–105: Feng Yu,/ Shutterstock.com, redstone/Shutterstock.com. Pages 106–107: Feng Yu/Shutterstock. com, KarSol/Shutterstock.com, Adam Parent/Shutterstock.com, redstone/ Shutterstock.com. Pages 114–115: Feng Yu/Shutterstock.com, redstone/Shutterstock. com, Everett Historical/Shutterstock.com. Pages 116–117: AlexandrBognat/ Shutterstock.com. Pages 128–129: Everett Historical/Shutterstock.com. Pages 142–143 Valentin Agapov/Shutterstock.com. Pages 144–145 Jiri Hera/Shutterstock. com. Pages 148–149 Jiri Hera/Shutterstock.com. Pages 154–155 Krasovski Dmitri/ Shutterstock.com. Back Cover: Pichet siritantiwat/Shutterstock.com

ISBN: 978-1-4197-3391-8

Printed and bound in China
10 9 8 7 6 5 4 3 2 1

Abrams Noterie products are available at special discounts when purchased in quantity for premiums and promotions as well as fundraising or educational use. Special editions can also be created to specification. For details, contact specialsales@abramsbooks.com or the address below.

Abrams Noterie® is a registered trademark of Harry N. Abrams, Inc.

ABRAMS The Art of Books
195 Broadway, New York, NY 10007
abramsbooks.com

MIX
Paper from
responsible sources
FSC™ C101537